Amongst Digital Humanists

Amongst Digital Humanists

An Ethnographic Study of Digital Knowledge Production

Smiljana Antonijević

palgrave
macmillan

First published 2015 by
PALGRAVE MACMILLAN

The author has asserted their right to be identified as the author of this work in accordance with the Copyright, Designs and Patents Act 1988.

Palgrave Macmillan in the UK is an imprint of Macmillan Publishers Limited, registered in England, company number 785998, of Houndmills, Basingstoke, Hampshire, RG21 6XS.

Palgrave Macmillan in the US is a division of Nature America, Inc., One New York Plaza, Suite 4500, New York, NY 10004-1562.

Palgrave Macmillan is the global academic imprint of the above companies and has companies and representatives throughout the world.

Hardback ISBN: 978–1–137–48417–8
E-PUB ISBN: 978–1–137–48419–2
E-PDF ISBN: 978–1–137–48418–5
DOI: 10.1057/9781137484185

Distribution in the UK, Europe and the rest of the world is by Palgrave Macmillan®, a division of Macmillan Publishers Limited, registered in England, company number 785998, of Houndmills, Basingstoke, Hampshire RG21 6XS.

Library of Congress Cataloging-in-Publication Data

Antonijevic, Smiljana, 1971–
    Amongst digital humanists : an ethnographic study of digital knowledge production / Smiljana Antonijevic.
       pages cm
    Includes bibliographical references and index.
    ISBN 978–1–137–48417–8 (alk. paper)
       1. Humanities—Data processing. 2. Humanities—Research—Data processing. 3. Humanities—Methodology. 4. Humanities—Electronic information resources. 5. Information storage and retrieval systems—Humanities. I. Title.

AZ105.A67 2015
001.30285—dc23   2015013097

A catalogue record of the book is available from the British Library.

To Goca and Miša

Contents

Figures

Acknowledgments

This book could not have been written without the participation and support of many people.

I am grateful to all the participants in this study, who contributed their time, effort, knowledge, and reflection. Their intellectual generosity enabled and inspired this study.

Several wonderful institutions and groups of colleagues contributed to this book:

The Royal Netherlands Academy of Arts and Sciences (KNAW) and the Andrew W. Mellon Foundation provided financial support for the research presented in the chapters.

Virtual Knowledge Studio for the Humanities and Social Sciences (VKS) of the KNAW was my intellectual home when the seed of this book had been planted and started to grow. I am thankful to all my VKS colleagues, and I am particularly indebted to Anne Beaulieu, Charles van den Heuvel, Paul Wouters, and Sally Wyatt.

The Alfalab team of the KNAW provided an expert network and knowledge infrastructure for a large part of this study. I am indebted to the Alfalab project leader Joris van Zundert and the entire Alfalab team.

Collaboration with the Oxford Internet Institute, the University of Amsterdam, and the Meertens Institute of the KNAW comprised the core of the projects *Humanities Information Practices* and *Digitizing Words of Power* that contributed to this study. I am grateful to all the colleagues from these projects, and particularly to Jacqueline Borsje.

Penn State University coordinated a project, *Digital Scholarly Workflow*, which provided a research infrastructure for the second part of the study presented in the book. I extend my thankfulness to all the project members, above all to Ellysa Stern Cahoy, who initiated and led this project.

My gratitude goes to the photographer Alice Teeple, who produced a series of wonderful ethnographic photographs as my fieldwork companion among the digital humanists, and to the Penn State University, which kindly allowed for a selection of the fieldwork photographs to be published in this book.

I owe special gratitude to Joris van Zundert, Charles van den Heuvel, Anne Beaulieu, and Jessica Elin who read the early drafts of this manuscript and provided valuable comments.

I am grateful to Charlene and William Woodcock III for generously lending me their rich experience in academic publishing.

I am indebted to the Illinois Institute of Technology Institute of Design for all the support during my final phases of working on this manuscript.

I am thankful to the editors and editorial assistants at Palgrave Macmillan for their dedicated efforts in the production of this book.

My special gratitude goes to my husband, Jeffrey Ubois, for his unceasing intellectual and emotional support.

Introduction

Transformations in scholarly practice and knowledge production have always been tightly linked to technological developments, reflecting a dialectical relationship in which technology, science, and scholarship continuously shape each other. Various fields of study, such as science and technology studies, history and philosophy of science, and anthropology of science and technology have explored this relationship, illuminating its manifold aspects. In recent years, these explorations have increasingly shifted toward digital technology and its relationship with contemporary scholarship.

The umbrella term "digital scholarship" encompasses various lines of thought and research on this subject: virtual knowledge (Wouters, Beaulieu, Scharnhorst, and Wyatt, 2013), e-research (Jankowski, 2009), e-science (Hine, 2006), cyberscience (Nentwich, 2003; Hine, 2008), etc. Numerous research streams examining disciplinary encounters with computational and digital technologies have emerged, including computational biology, computational chemistry, medical informatics, and digital geology, to name just a few.

Digital scholarship has also become part of those academic disciplines where practices of knowledge production have traditionally been considered detached from technology—the humanities and social sciences. Digital humanities, as the encounter between digital technologies and humanities is now commonly called,[1] has burgeoned into a substantial field of both practice and study. Although the concept of digital humanities goes back decades (see Hockey, 2004), a wider adoption of digital tools and methods in the humanities is a relatively recent development. Describing the landscape of digital humanities, Svensson (2010) emphasizes a "surge of activity in the multifarious emerging field often referred to as 'digital humanities'" (para. 1), where humanists' engagement with technology significantly intensified and diversified over the last few years.

The present book delves into this burgeoning and widely diversified field, seeking to illustrate how ethnographic analysis of scholarly practice can cast a better understanding of the complexities of digital knowledge production. While drawing on previous work in digital humanities, this book emphasizes rich empirical data gathered in my three-year-long fieldwork among digital humanists and their changing scholarly environment.

Transformations arising from humanists' engagement with technology as embodied in objects, activities, and in ways of knowing (see Bijker, Hughes, and Pinch, 2012) included shifts in research practices, knowledge, and legitimacy claims, as well as in widening expectations and fears regarding such changing scholarly landscape. New digital tools, resources, and methods for humanities research emerged, along with innovative academic organizational structures and career paths, such as digital humanities centers and alternative academic careers. Social media and other forms of online scholarly communication became part of "normal science," paving the way to some still-contested "departures from normal science," such as open peer review, participatory knowledge production, and crowdfunded science. Collaborative and interdisciplinary efforts in the humanities expanded, together with multimodal digital publishing platforms and projects. New academic programs appeared, offering degrees in digital humanities, digital knowledge, and similar subjects, raising new generations of humanities scholars.

With the growth and diversification of humanists' engagement with digital technologies, struggles between reproduction and transformation of scholarly practices and assumptions became increasingly visible, spawning challenges between "the established holders of the legitimacy of discourse and the new contenders," as Bourdieu puts it (see Wacquant, 1989: 37). Vigorous debates emerged focusing on methodological and epistemological premises of humanities scholarship in general and digital humanities in particular. Questions included academic identity and the future of humanities scholarship, distribution of resources between traditional and digital scholarship, and integration of digital humanities into the curriculum and credit system of traditional humanities.

Debates about legitimacy, authority, and scope also arose in the field of digital humanities, following the growth of this community and the overall uptake of digital technologies in the humanities. Many questions arose: Who is "in" and who is "out" of the community of digital humanists? What constitutes digital humanities work, and what does not? How broad are the disciplinary, methodological, and cultural spheres of digital humanities? What is the relationship between theoretical and applied aspects of digital humanities? These and similar questions started permeating the field, as I discuss comprehensively in chapter 1.

In contrast to an abundance of theoretical disciplinary debates, analytical lenses turned less frequently toward the empirical studies of humanists' engagement with digital technologies. A number of studies looked at specific areas and patterns of technology use in the humanities, such as information-seeking behavior, data management, and archiving. Those studies provided valuable insights although of somewhat narrower scope, as they mostly focused on discrete activities and problems. A smaller number of studies empirically analyzed humanists' work as integrated practice of digital knowledge production, observed from sociological, philosophical, anthropological, or the perspective of science and technology studies. Yet, scholarly interest and need for studies of that kind continued to increase. For instance, Svensson (2010) called for the examination of humanists' digital work from the perspective of individual scholars' daily practices, and Kirschenbaum (2014) similarly argued for the analysis of digital humanities in action.

This particular approach—studying integrated practices of digital knowledge production in the humanities from the ethnographic perspective—guided my research and formed the empirical foundation of this book. The research was conducted from 2010 to 2013 at 23 educational, research, and funding institutions in the United States and Europe. It involved 258 participants, including researchers, faculty, students, university administrators, librarians, software developers, policy makers, and funders. Through case studies, surveys, in-depth interviews, and observations, the study sought to highlight issues relevant to understanding digital scholarship in the humanities at three levels: the micro level (individual scholars), the meso level (academic fields), and the macro level (academic organizations). This three-part analytical structure brought to light the complexity of digital knowledge production in the humanities, demonstrating that the core of comparative studies is indeed "to make sense of differences, not collapse them" (Strathern, 1987: 286). At the same time, in-depth interviews with the study participants and prolonged observations of their work enabled insights into more personal, subtle, and affective aspects of those professional engagements. From junior scholars explaining their own possessiveness of information, or "data territoriality," in the context of tenure-track efforts, to senior scholars describing their struggles as "techno-dinosaurs" in the digital age, these personal accounts illuminated aspects of scholarly work that are too often sidelined in larger theoretical discussions. A detailed account of the methodological framework and premises of the research is provided in chapter 1.

My primary purpose was to illustrate how ethnographic examination of scholarly practice contributes to a better understanding of the complexities of digital knowledge production. Any appearance of favoring either side of the debate about digital humanities, or of widening the gap between opposing perspectives, is unintentional. I offer this qualification in light of Bourdieu's (1988) caution, "There is no escaping the work of constructing the object, and the responsibility that it entails. There is no object [of study] that does not imply a viewpoint" (p. 6).

My viewpoint on the object of study analyzed in this book evolved gradually over the course of my research engagement in four academic projects—*Alfalab: eHumanities Tools and Resources*,[2] a project of the Royal Netherlands Academy of Arts

Figure 0.1 In a scholar's office.
Source: Alice Teeple, Penn State University.

and Sciences (KNAW); *Digitizing Words of Power*,[3] a collaborative endeavor between the KNAW and the University of Amsterdam; *Humanities Information Practices*,[4] a partnership of the KNAW, Oxford Internet Institute, and University College London; and *Digital Scholarly Workflow*,[5] an Andrew W. Mellon foundation–funded project of Penn State University.

These four projects informed the overall research and composed the intellectual background of this book. The empirical data primarily drew on *Alfalab* and *Digital Scholarly Workflow* projects, forming an integrated ethnographic study I conducted over a period of three years.

Alfalab, or *HumanitiesLab*, was a collaborative project of six KNAW research institutes, realized between 2009 and 2011. This project had a threefold goal: (1) to establish an interdisciplinary digital humanities research network within the KNAW; (2) to create a knowledge base of best practices in digital humanities at national and international levels; and (3) to develop a set of prototype tools for three kinds of humanities research—text analysis, historical GIS, and historical population counts.

Within *Alfalab*, I was one of the three researchers in the research group called *InterfaceLab*,[6] which, as the name suggests, served as the interface among various disciplinary groups within the project, as well as a liaison with the outside partners of *Alfalab*. Interdisciplinary work is never a straightforward task, and it develops a specifically challenging edge when focused on innovative research areas such as digital humanities. *InterfaceLab* was thus established as part of the *Alfalab* project, equidistant from all other partners. It connected participating scholars by developing reflexive cross-disciplinary understanding among them, and by implementing those reflexive feedback cycles in the project development. From the outset, we talked often with our *Alfalab* collaborators, prompting reflections on epistemological, methodological, or other discoveries and challenges encountered in practice. We focused on developing a common vocabulary among the team members, uncovering and deliberating methodological and epistemological differences, facilitating collaborative production of various outputs (academic papers, databases, presentations, blog posts, and so on), and supporting shared values. *InterfaceLab* can thus be seen as a forerunner of the approach that Liu (2014) recently proposed arguing that interdisciplinary teams focused on digital knowledge in the humanities should include at least one ethnographer who would analyze and facilitate the team's dynamics.

In supporting tool development, *InterfaceLab* organized and promoted user involvement from the earliest phases, ensuring that their input systematically informed the tool design process. One of our goals was to assist scholars in articulating their discipline-specific methods and research objects in a way that best informed the design process. We also worked on cultivating researchers' openness to potential new ways of working. On the design side, we collaborated with our colleagues from the tool development team on procedures for advanced interfacing between different kinds of scholarly work. Among users and designers, we facilitated reflexive examination of research practices and knowledge production in digital settings.

Looking beyond our team, we listened to voices from the field, harvesting best practices from other projects and institutions. We also contributed to professional debates, sharing our knowledge, experiences and approach. Our goal was to simultaneously support interaction within the community of practice while promoting critical reflection on research methods in digital humanities. Supporting interaction in the community of practice also assumed developing collaborative endeavors. As part of *Alfalab*, I thus participated in two interdisciplinary and inter-institutional projects—*Digitizing Words of Power* and *Humanities Information Practices* (HIP).

The *HIP* project, funded by the Research Information Network, was carried out in 2010 and it examined information behavior and collaborative practices of humanities scholars. Focusing on six case studies, the project explored how humanists integrate digital and non-digital resources in their work, as well as how they find, create, analyze, organize, manage, and communicate research data and materials. The research provided insights into a range of practices, experiences, and approaches in humanists' research and interaction with digital technologies, as well as into some of the main challenges and barriers to the adoption of digital scholarship in humanities work. Based on those findings, this project identified trends relevant in contemporary humanities digital scholarship, and provided a set of policy recommendations for potential use of research funders and institutions.

Digitizing Words of Power, funded by the KNAW and the Netherlands Organisation for Scientific Research, was also conducted during 2010, and it brought together an interdisciplinary team developing tools and corpora for philological research. The team gathered philologists, ethnologists, ethnographers, computer scientists, and experts in science and technology studies to link their skills and expertise. Such interdisciplinary projects, combining social sciences and the humanities on one the hand, and computer sciences on the other, have largely been the

---

result of policy-led initiatives. *Digitizing Words of Power* project, by contrast, was a bottom-up initiative. It emerged when researchers from different fields recognized the potential of crossing disciplinary boundaries to support their individual and collective research. The humanists working on this project had neither previous experience in digital humanities nor knowledge of the digital tools and methods developed for humanities research. Yet, like their disciplinary forerunner Roberto Busa, they shared a strong aspiration to enrich their work through engagement with technology and interdisciplinary collaboration. This was accomplished through regular team meetings where both humanistic and technological aspects of the project were discussed, facilitating interdisciplinary trust and knowledge. For instance, an important segment of the teamwork centered on thinking through how the various sources to be digitized would be used in research, which kinds of questions would be generated, and so on. We wanted to do more than simply "digitize," in the usual sense of the term. Our goal was to build a digital resource shaped by research practices that closely linked data with interpretation.

Building a digital resource closely linked to humanists' scholarly practice was one of the core points of the *Digital Scholarly Workflow*, in which I had the role of the principal research anthropologist investigator. The first phase of this project, funded by the Andrew W. Mellon Foundation, was carried out at Pennsylvania State University (Penn State) between 2012–2013; the second phase, also funded by Mellon, is currently underway and runs through 2016 as a collaborative endeavor of Penn State and George Mason University. This project focuses on scholars' information behavior at all stages of the research lifecycle with the goal of developing software and service architecture to support that behavior. In the first phase, the project documented and analyzed practices and needs related to digital scholarly workflow, particularly in the humanities, pointing at gaps in existing tools, services, and infrastructures. The aim was to inform future development of an online scholarly workflow and to facilitate the development of literacies for humanists' information management needs. The second phase of the project is devoted to developing a digital research tool for humanities scholarship using *Zotero* as a test platform, in collaboration with the Roy Rosenzweig Center for History and New Media. A more detailed methodological account of this and other three projects that informed the research presented in this book is provided in chapter 1.

Chapter 1 sets out context for understanding the theoretical and methodological framework of the key concepts and arguments presented in this book. This chapter opens with a brief chronology of digital humanities, outlining the early days of humanities computing, and identifying the most relevant debates and controversies challenging digital humanities today. The chapter then turns to casting an ethnographic look on digital humanities, proposing the methodological and epistemological transition from examination of digital humanities to the analysis of digital humanists.

Chapter 2 analyzes how individual scholars across disciplines engage with digital technologies in their research workflows. It examines practices, needs, and challenges of scholars' interaction with digital tools and methods at different stages of the research lifecycle. The chapter harvests a comparative multidisciplinary perspective of the research, illuminating specificities of humanists' practices in the context of digital scholarship.

Chapter 3 traces four components of scholarly transformation and capacity building concerning humanists' engagement with digital technologies: research capacity, knowledge capacity, value capacity, and technical capacity. The chapter examines how these aspects of capacity building interrelate with disciplinary objects and methods of inquiry, evaluation of scholarly results, collaborative work, and the design of digital research tools.

Chapter 4, the third and final empirical section of the book, explores the practices and challenges of (re)organizing humanities' academic activities, research units, services, and administrative hierarchies with respect to digital scholarship. Specifically, it considers a set of organizational practices related to digital humanities centers; alternative academic tracks for "hybrid" scholars; organizational support for technologically intensive research; infrastructural and financial sustainability of digital infrastructures and related issues.

In conclusion, chapter 5 juxtaposes the empirical findings and theoretical approaches discussed in the previous four chapters through analytical frameworks of boundary work and socio-technical expectations. The chapter proposes an analytical delineation between digital humanities and digital scholarship in the humanities as a prologue to rethinking a set of disciplinary, educational, funding, and organizational questions regarding humanities transition toward digital scholarship, and it argues for the pluralistic future of digital knowledge production in the humanities.

CHAPTER 1

Digital Humanities as Theory and Practice

In his recent text on the meaning of the digital humanities, Liu (2013, p. 409) argued that an ethnographer of this field "might take a page from Claude Lévi-Strauss and chart the current digital humanities as something like a grid of affiliations and differences between neighboring tribes". Indeed, complex social grids and seemingly fuzzy practices—analogous to those in contemporary digital humanities—constitute the ethnographer's epistemic atelier in which different forms and norms of social behavior coalesce in an articulated arrangement. The articulation emerges through narratives of the fieldwork data and the ethnographer's metanarrative of these empirical accounts.

The empirical narratives and analytical metanarratives presented in this study construct, each in its own way, a story about digital humanities. More precisely, they tell *one of the possible* stories about humanities knowledge production in the digital age. There are many other stories that can be, have been, and will be told on the same subject. Some of them will uphold each other, while others will take adversarial positions. Competing scholarly discourses revolve around three general questions—which phenomena are worth of investigation, how should they be methodologically approached, and what do the results of those investigations mean (see Gross, 1990). Such professional debates sometimes turn into fierce power struggles in the increasingly competitive academic environment of today, in which individuals, disciplines, and institutions vie for resources and socioeconomic positioning amid the turn toward neoliberal university (see Canaan and Shumar, 2008; Gill, 2009). Those struggles constitute an important element of the socio-epistemic environment in which contemporary scholarly endeavors, including digital humanities, take place. The arena of digital humanities thus changes in response to the internal debates, as well as in response to the external undercurrents that shape its broader course.

This chapter starts with a brief chronology of the field of digital humanities, and then turns to discussing some of the most persistent controversies in this field. This review of digital humanities as theory then unfolds into a proposition for exploring digital humanities as practice, seen through the ethnographic lens. The concluding part of this chapter outlines the methodological design of the study presented in this book, providing the context for the empirical narratives of digital knowledge production in the humanities delineated in the consequent chapters.

A Brief Chronology of Digital Humanities

The concept of digital humanities reaches back decades, into still uncharted history of humanities' engagement with computing (see Nyhan et al., 2013). Yet, the founding story of digital humanities is generally associated with one perhaps unlikely source of scholarly innovation—a Jesuit priest. In 1949, Roberto Busa, the Italian priest, commonly thought of as "the father of digital humanities," undertook the ambitious task of indexing the complete works of St. Thomas Aquinas. He realized that computational technologies could not only help in his task, but also change the entire nature of the endeavor.

Throughout the 1950s and 1960s, the use of computation in linguistics and literary studies gained recognition, leading to important early publications such as Lord's (1958) statistical study of literary style, Morton's (1965) scientific solution to authorship, and Russel's (1967) word count and concordance generator. Pioneering academic journals and research centers followed. The

Centre for Literary and Linguistic Computing at Cambridge was launched in 1963 and the *Computers and the Humanities* journal published its first edition in 1966. These innovative efforts inspired broader developments during the 1970s and 1980s, leading to new academic journals and societies, as well as to academic conferences dedicated to the field, which at the time was known as "humanities computing."

For decades, humanities computing focused on the encounter between computing and two humanities disciplines—linguistics and literary studies. The names of the journals, research centers, and professional associations founded during this time illustrate this specific orientation, specifically, Association for Literary and Linguistic Computing, *Literary and Linguistic Computing* journal, and the Centre for Literary and Linguistic Computing. Somewhat broader in scope was the International Conference on Computing in the Humanities conference series, which led to the formation of the Association for Computers and the Humanities in 1978, an organization that incorporated computational methods and approaches in other humanities disciplines, such as music, archeology, and art. Yet, as Hockey (2004) notices, those efforts "continued to concentrate on literary and linguistic computing, with some emphasis on 'linguistic'" (para 19).

Linguistic and literary computing continued to dominate the field during the 1970s and 1980s. This focus is evident in the most prominent initiatives and projects of the time, including *Project Gutenberg* digital library launched in 1971; *Thesaurus Linguae Graecae* research center and digital collection established in 1972; *Oxford Text Archive* of literary and language resources founded in 1976; *Women Writers Project* organized in 1986; *Perseus Project* collections of Greco-Roman classics started in 1987; and *Text Encoding Initiative* for standardized encoding of electronic text also initiated in 1987.

Throughout the 1980s and 1990s, the use of digital technologies in humanists' work expanded beyond the community of humanities computing. This new expansion resulted from technological developments, specifically personal computing in the 1980s and the creation of the Internet and World Wide Web in the 1990s. The main areas of humanists' uptake of digital technologies were similar to

Figure 1.1 The preeminence of personal computing.

that of other academic disciplines, and predominantly included Word processing and computer-mediated communication.[1]

With these developments, digital technologies became more accessible to individual scholars and their work turned increasingly portable and interconnected, linking activities of finding information, writing, communicating, and other segments of the scholarly workflow. The emergence of the World Wide Web generated another important and innovative opportunity for both individual scholars and institutions: self-publishing. The ability to easily present and distribute scholarly materials online became one of the primary interests and activities in humanities computing during the 1990s. A significant number of initiatives concentrated on creating digital collections[2] and publishing them online. This work included cornerstone projects such as the *Rossetti Archive*, initiated in 1993; the *William Blake Archive* and *David Rumsey Map Collection*, both started in 1996; the *Cuneiform*

Digital Library Initiative of 1998; and the *Women Writers Online* project which first appeared online in 1999.

This emphases on delivering digitized materials online continued and expanded into the new millennium, across commercial and noncommercial sectors, generating extensive online resources such as *Google Books, Europeana, World Digital Library Project, Digital Public* and *Library of America*, to name a few.

The appearance of blogging platforms and academic open access electronic journals in the 1990s transformed digital scholarship even further, instigating major changes in scholarly communication and publishing. Throughout the 2000s, academic blogging burgeoned, alongside other Web 2.0 platforms, such as YouTube, Twitter, and Flickr. Open access electronic publishing also flourished, ushering in open peer review, open annotation, and other significant scholarly developments. Participatory knowledge production boomed, elevating sources such as Wikipedia to equal footing with traditional modes of knowledge production and opening the door to crowdsourced projects such as *Phila Place, Ancient Lives, Civic Epistemologies*, and the like.

The multimedia methods and content launched in the 1990s expanded in the twenty-first century, propelled by broadband Internet access, sophisticated image and sound processing capabilities, and affordable data storage. 3D modeling and virtual environments advanced as well, eventually morphing into new form of hybrid materiality exemplified in 3D printing. All of these technological developments strongly shaped humanists' work, resulting in projects such as *Hypecities, Virtual Qumran, Mapping the Republic of Letters*, and so on.

It is impossible to do more in a brief chronology than to chart, in very broad strokes, some of the main socio-technical innovations and corresponding developments in the humanities digital knowledge production. Yet, even this cursory overview illustrates the extensive growth and diversification in humanists' dealings with digital technologies over the past 60 years. This exponential change brought new challenges to humanities computing, giving rise to conceptual, normative, and organizational questions and controversies.

Controversies in Digital Humanities

Naming the Field

Since inception in the 1950s, the field recognized today as digital humanities underwent numerous transformations, including its name. Huggett (2012) remarks that the term "literary computing" peaked in the 1980s and declined in the mid-1990s, when *humanities computing* and *linguist computing* took prominence. The term "digital humanities" came last to the scene, in the mid-1990s, but by the year 2005 it was the dominant term for the discipline (ibid.). Vanhoutte (2013) makes a similar terminological distinction, using the term humanities computing to refer to "the practice of using computing *for* and *in* the humanities from the early 1950s to 2004 when 'Digital Humanities' became the prominent name for the field" (p. 120; italics in the original).

One theory suggests that this discursive shift from the term humanities computing to digital humanities indicated the field's coming of age, its maturation as a fully developed professional and intellectual area of scholarship (Hayles, 2012). Another argument describes a more practical and strategic reason behind the name change. Kirschenbaum (2012) traces this terminological shift to a specific discussion about the title for a Blackwell *Companion to Digital Humanities*, published in 2004, after the initial title *Companion to Digitized Humanities* was rejected as too narrowly focused on digitization. Another milestone in the naming of the field occurred in 2005, when the Association for Literary and Linguistic Computing and the Association for Computers and the Humanities merged into the Alliance of Digital Humanities Organizations (ADHO).[3] When the US National Endowment for the Humanities launched their funding initiative, Digital Humanities Initiative, in 2006[4] they chose this title over "ehumanities" and "humanities computing." Most recently, the discursive victory of the term digital humanities manifested in the name-change of the longest–standing journal in the field, *Literary and Linguistic Computing*, renamed *Digital Scholarship in the Humanities* as of 2015.[5]

Collectively, these events reaffirmed digital humanities as the main designator for the field. But even though digital humanities gained a discursive dominance over the term humanities computing, the relationship between epistemic and methodological assumptions underlying these two designators remained complex (see Svensson, 2009). A number of authors thus pose the question of "whether the discursive transition from humanities computing to digital humanities is mainly a matter of repackaging (humanities computing), or whether the new label also indicates an expanded scope" (ibid., para. 37).

Defining the field

This terminological turmoil indicated other controversies that have started to haunt the field, revolving around the identity of digital humanities and digital humanists. The complexity of this identity apprehension is illustrated in various, as yet unresolved, attempts at defining the field of digital humanities.

Thaller (2012) observes that, after five decades of development, the field has reached a consensus "that there is a shadowy subject between these disciplinary worlds [humanities and computing]" (p. 8), and that defining digital humanities is more difficult today than it was 50 years ago, since the number of possibilities to label something as digital humanities rose steeply.

Alvarado (2011) similarly suggests an honest disclosure that there is no definition of digital humanities, "if by definition we mean a consistent set of theoretical concerns and research methods that might be aligned with a given discipline" (para. 1). Svesson (2010) posits that digital humanities "defies any precise definition and that it can hardly be called a discipline" (para. 20), adding that it is questionable whether this area of scholarship even constitutes a field.

Kirschenbaum (2014) goes even further in asserting ontological uncertainty about digital humanities. Unlike Svesson, however, he describes it in positive terms: "We will never know what digital humanities 'is' because we don't want to know nor is it useful for us to know," he concludes (p. 15). Huggett (2012) similarly observes that digital humanities has been operating with "almost as many different definitions as there are scholars" (p. 87), but for him this is indicative of a situation in which the humanities side of the field is left undefined, encompassed in broad references to interdisciplinarity and big tents.

Determining the scope of the field

Huggett's observation brings to light an additional challenge in digital humanities, which is determining the scope of the field and its relation to traditional humanities disciplines. While digital humanities potentially operates across the humanities fields, in practice its scope is more narrowly focused on a subset of disciplines, and textual orientation continues to be one of its core features. Digital humanities's close connection with literary studies and linguistics generates a more problematic relationship with other disciplines (see Svensson, 2012; Hugget, 2012). To illustrate this point, Huggett parallels the development of digital humanities and digital archeology, showing that these two fields have rarely coalesced, despite sharing similar assumptions and goals.

In the same manner, Svensson (2009) argues that strong textual alignment of digital humanities and methodological orientation on text encoding and analysis limit the scope of the field's penetration and uptake in many other humanities disciplines. Fitzpatrick (2012) similarly observes that digital humanities, as a continuation of humanities computing, "results in projects that focus on computing methods applicable to textual materials," yet she remarks that such a focus, although typical, is "far from exclusive" (p. 13).

Indeed, the field of digital humanities has advanced in such a way that its textual angle, though still predominant, is certainly not exclusive. McPherson (2009) thus proposes a typology of digital humanities that differentiates among computing humanities, blogging humanities, and multimodal humanities, with the last category particularly emphasizing audiovisual and other multimodal forms. Davidson (2008) similarly distinguishes between digital humanities 1.0 and 2.0, with the second phase promoting a wider scope of the field. By contrast, Svensson (2010) raises a cautionary voice:

> In practice, it would seem that humanities computing (even if called digital humanities) will not—at least not fully or anytime soon—become the multimodal humanities or humanities 2.0 envisioned in these articles [MacPherson's and Davidson's].

Ethnocentrism

Textual emphasis in digital humanities, including the methodological dominance of linguistic and literary studies, is discussed more and more frequently in relation to the cultural dominance of the English language and the Anglo-American culture. "Is there a non Anglo-American Digital Humanities (DH), and if so, what are its characteristics?" Fiormonte (2012, p. 59) asks. He goes on to suggest that although non–Anglo-American digital humanities projects do exist, they are neither as frequent nor as visible as those representing the America-Canada-United Kingdom axis:

> Even though so much effort has been expended in making existing DH associations and organizations more international, the impression remains the same: a solid Anglo-American stem onto which several individuals of mostly European countries are grafted. (p. 64)

This observation finds support in Terras's (2012) global survey of digital humanities centers, which shows that of the 114 centers across 24 countries two thirds are located in three countries—the United States, Canada, and the United Kingdom—and only one-third in the remaining 21 countries. Fiormonte concludes that this data shows the subordinate position of non–English-speaking digital humanists, and posits that the geopolitical unbalance and the economic interests "operate at the heart of the DH system" (Terras, p. 62).

Similar arguments resonate in the growing interest in postcolonial digital humanities. Consonantly with Fiormonte's above-cited question, McPherson (2012) asks "Why are the digital humanities so white?" discussing the issue of race in the field. The interest in postcolonial digital humanities is also evidenced in the number of initiatives taking shape at both institutional and cross-institutional levels. For example, Digital Humanities Focal Group at Stanford University aspires to counteract the English-language dominance in digital humanities, while Global Outlook: Digital Humanities, a special interest group of the ADHO, facilitates communication and collaboration among digital humanities researchers in high-, mid-, and low-income economies.

Who is In and Who is Out

In addition to disciplinary, cultural, and economic distinctions within digital humanities, debates about the professional profile and scope of the field also exist. Numerous debates and disagreements about how to define the field speak to these challenges. On the one hand, the field of digital humanities tends to be broadly described as a set of practices coexisting under a "big tent." For instance, one of the field's flagship journals, *Digital Humanities Quarterly*, describes digital humanities as "a diverse and still emerging field that encompasses the practice of humanities research in and through information technology" (DHQ, "About"). Svesson (2010) similarly suggests that the concept of digital humanities should not be used as a designator of a well-defined field, but instead as "an inclusive notion that will allow us to talk about different kinds of initiatives and activities in the intersection between the humanities and information technology" (para. 12)

Contradicting these inclusionary approaches are those arguing for in group/out group differentiation. Determining "who's in, who's out" is the second big struggle of a developing field, which follows in the footsteps of the initial definitional struggles (see Kirschenbaum, 2014:10). Indeed, delineations by negation—what does *not* constitute digital humanities work and who is *not* in the field—have followed other discursive disputes in this area of humanities scholarship, beginning with the shift away from humanities computing and continuing forward.

For instance, Unsworth's (2002) text *What Is Humanities Computing and What Is Not?* argued that although a computer as a general purpose machine can be used for different scholarly proposes, only a subset of these activities can be considered humanities computing, namely those "in which the computer is used as tool for modeling humanities data and our understanding of it" (para. 4). In his account, the importance of clarifying what *is* and what is *not* humanities computing is twofold. First, doing so helps scholars distinguish between authentic humanities computing and possible "charlatans," as he puts it. Second, this differentiation helps justify resource allocation and investment, such as project funding, new academic units, and degrees (ibid.).

Unsworth's words echo even among contemporary scholars who promote more inclusive understanding of the field. For instance, Fitzpatrick (2010) offers a broad and inclusive definition of digital humanities (see p. 12), but also makes a point of stating what digital humanities is not:

> Should [we] throw open the floodgates and declare all forms of humanities scholarship that come into contact with the digital to be digital humanities? Should we expand the definition of the field to include... "every medievalist with a website"? Undoubtedly not. (p. 14)

Who should or should not be included in the field is also the theme of Ramsay's MLA 2011 paper *Who's In and Who is Out*. He opens with the observation that digital humanities "has most recently tended to welcome anyone and anything" (par. 2), and then proposes two criteria for determining who qualifies as a digital humanist and who does not. Simply put, these criteria are (1) knowing how to code, and (2) making things. Ramsay explains:

> If you are not making anything, you are not... a digital humanist. You might be something else that is good and worthy—maybe you're a scholar of new media, or maybe a game theorist, or maybe a classicist with a blog—but if you aren't building, you are not engaged in the "methodologization" of the humanities, which, to me, is the hallmark of the discipline. (para. 9)

The same approach to defining digital humanities can be found in Burdick et al.'s (2012) guide to digital humanities, under the checklist, *What Isn't the Digital Humanities?* Burdick and her coauthors argue that non-digital humanities work can be identified based on the following criteria:

> The mere use of digital tools for the purpose of humanistic research and communication does not qualify as Digital Humanities. Nor... is Digital Humanities to be understood as the study of digital artifacts, new media, or contemporary culture in place of physical artifacts, old media, or historical culture. (p. 122)

The authors also suggest an "advisory list" of core competencies in digital humanities, that is, the essential skills aspiring digital humanists should master (p. 132). These skill sets include technical, intellectual, and administrative competencies, with an emphasis on technical competencies. Namely, the authors identify 12 core technical competencies, compared to only three competencies comprising intellectual and administrative skills. This advisory list is additionally problematic in its framing of technical and intellectual skills as separate, unrelated competencies. Overlooking the synergy between technical and intellectual skills in digital humanities raises a "Where's the beef?" argument (see Scheinfeldt, 2010) and questions the interpretative capabilities of cultural criticism in digital humanities (see Liu, 2012), as I discuss later in this chapter.

Debates about the scope and boundaries of digital humanities referenced here are addressed again, and with suggested potential resolutions, in the concluding chapter of this book. From the detailed discussion in chapter 5 we understandthat while defining an academic field is a legitimate effort, doing so through the boundary work (see Gieryn, 1983; Bowker and Star, 1999; Carlile, 2002) framed around exclusionary discourses raises a number of obstacles and questions. Such an approach discourages potential new members, and imposes provisional, rigid categories that preclude alternative lines of work. Furthermore, it adds to the resistance that some of the traditionally trained scholars already exhibit toward digital humanities (see chapters 3 and 4). Additional concerns arise from assertions that scholars using digital technologies for "basic" scholarly activities are not part of the community of digital humanists. Repeated calls for humanists to embrace the benefits of digital tools and methods cannot be received positively if scholars' initial uptake of these tools is assessed as inadequate for the entrance to the field. As Liu (2012) puts it,

> Mainstream humanists have come to recognize that, at minimum, they need a search function to do research; and the nature of digital media is such that the transition from the minimum to the maximum is almost instantaneous. (p. 494)

Furthermore, if significant funds are granted to digital humanities initiatives based on their pledge to achieve wider impact within the humanities community, how can those investments be justified unless they are spread evenly to include both technologically advanced and less advanced disciplines and scholars? Closely related is the question which disciplinary authority determines whether a certain type of scholars' engagement with technology does or does not constitute a contribution to the humanities digital knowledge production. Finally, if researchers using digital technologies for "basic" scholarly activities are excluded from the community of digital humanists, then their perspective and input on the development of digital research tools, methods, and resources will be excluded, too.

The problems of exclusionary discourse are recognized in the community of digital humanists, often by the same authors who contributed to that discourse. In a recent text, Ramsay (2013) examines the sources of rancor in the digital humanities debates. He proposes that there are two core types of digital humanities—DH Types I and II—and that the arguments arise from confusing the two types. He goes on to clarify that his often-cited observation about the importance of building in digital humanities actually represents DH I, not DH II. Ramsay concludes that a bitter ideological war between practitioners of DH I and DH II will continue "as long as the term 'digital humanities' continues to mean several different (sometimes contradictory) things."

Similarly, Unsworth, in his 2010 address to the Digital Humanities Summer Institute, argues that dogmatic and exclusionary approaches in digital humanities need to be debunked and opened to different types of scholarly interpretation and work. Reflecting on young scholars' struggle to classify their work in the face of rigid orthodoxies of the field, Unsworth recognizes the resulting academic risk, and, to his credit, acknowledges his role in creating the problem:

> This orthodoxy is unfortunate, in my view, and yet...I think I need to take some responsibility for the situation I'm describing....If I'm 'fessing up, I would also need to mention—in connection with the orthodoxy—an article called "What is Humanities Computing and What is Not?" published in 2002. (p. 11)

Unsworth points out that scholars who do not think of themselves as "insiders" in the digital humanities community nonetheless enthusiastically engage with digital technologies in their
work. He thus argues that the field, in order to expand, must be
inclusive:

> We're going to need to reward the people who think of creative
> ways to apply digital tools and methods in the humanities, rather
> than worrying about whether, in so doing, they are doing "digital
> humanities." (p. 18)

I return to discussing these important issues in chapter 5, where I
propose an analytical distinction between digital humanities and
digital scholarship in the humanities and argue for a pluralistic
future of digital knowledge production in the humanities.

Where Is the Beef and Where Is the Money

The debates about the scope and inclusion in digital humanities
evolve into discussions about the field's methodological and epistemological commitments and contributions. One of the important questions in this debate is to what extent digital humanities
offer new arguments, research questions, and potential answers,
or whether novelty of its manner may camouflage for triteness of
subject, to paraphrase Hume.

Formulated as a question "Where's the beef?" Scheinfeldt
(2010) posits that, after a deluge of new tools, the field of digital humanities needs to articulate what arguments does it make,
and what questions it answers that could not be answered before.
Scheinfeldt suggests that the field has not been theoretically
strong enough and that it underperformed in terms of generating
and answering research questions, which is the reason for concern. Digital humanities should thus adapt to include both theoretical work, focused on raising arguments and questions, and on
activities of building tools and resources (ibid.).

Indeed, the examples cited in the previous section, which origi-
nate from established authorities in the field—Unsworth, Ramsay,
Burdick and colleagues—portray digital humanities as an applied

field of building and modeling, where, ironically, study of the resulting digital artifacts remains beyond the field's scope. In other words, while digital humanists build and use tools, studying those tools and/or how people interact with them is not necessarily part of their inquiry. This line of reasoning is problematic as it disassociates digital artifacts from their developers and users. It suggests that even when artifacts do have politics, as Winner famously put it, those politics rest in somebody else's epistemic yard. This approach, as I elaborate throughout this book, is detrimental to every type of digital scholarship, including humanities. Unless academics turn their analytical lenses toward digital research tools and resources they will lose understanding and influence over the epistemic texture of these artifacts that shape both what and how scholars know. Digital humanists should indeed develop coding and other digital skills, but for more meaningful purposes than passively using digital artifacts. These skills are critical to humanists becoming competent analysts and commentators of digital artifacts and their impact on scholarly work.

Drucker (2012) argues for an integrated approach of moving beyond the "theory/making" dichotomy, toward a synthesis of doing as thinking. "The challenge is to shift humanistic study from attention to the *effects* of technology (from readings of social media, games, narrative, personae, digital texts, images, environments), to a humanistically informed theory of the *making* of technology (a humanistic computing at the level of design, modeling of information architecture, data types, interfaces, and protocols)" (p. 87; italics in the original). This is an interesting position insomuch that it argues for the integration of theory and practice—a long-standing approach in sociology, anthropology, science and technology studies—yet it proposes a reversal of key epistemic commitments held in these fields. While these disciplines pursue the integrated approach as heuristic concerning the effects and responsibilities arising from social construction of technical artifacts, Drucker advises humanists to shift their attention away from effects. Furthermore, it is paradoxical that digital humanities, as the field that prides itself upon its interdisciplinary character, intentionally excludes closely related and highly relevant areas of study, such as new media, Internet studies, or game theory and overlooks important bodies of work in philosophy of science and similar disciplines.

For a newcomer to digital humanities, such an approach would probably seem peculiar, as it runs counter the backbone of humanistic thought—namely, criticism. Yet, as Liu (2012) illustrates, the field of digital humanities has been "noticeably missing in action on the cultural-critical scene" throughout decades of its existence. Socioeconomic, cultural, political, and similar questions have rarely been raised in the field. The same applies to more technologically oriented issues, such as digital divide or privacy, extensively discussed in New Media and similar fields. As Liu puts is:

> It is as if... digital humanists just concentrate on pushing the "execute" button on projects that amass the most data for the greatest number, process that data most efficiently and flexibly (flexible efficiency being the hallmark of postindustrialism), and manage the whole through ever "smarter" standards, protocols, schema, templates, and databases uplifting Frederick Winslow Taylor's original scientific industrialism into ultraflexible postindustrial content management system camouflaged as digital editions, libraries, and archives—all without pausing to reflect on the relation of the whole digital juggernaut to the new world order. (p. 491)

Liu further argues that the field's lack of cultural criticism will hinder its wider recognition, as well as the integration of digital and traditional humanities. Eventually, it will impede the possibility of digital humanities becoming an advocate of humanities in the increasingly difficult neoliberal academic environment, which is the role Liu holds digital humanities should have.

Not everyone agrees with this view. For instance, Chun (2014) argues that the biggest flaw of digital humanities is exactly its self-appointed role as the "savior" of humanities. "I want to propose," Chun affirms, "that the dark side of the digital humanities is its bright side, its alleged promise to save the humanities by making them and their graduates relevant, by giving their graduates technical skills that will allow them to thrive in a difficult and precarious job market" (p. 2). The author draws attention to the uncritical embrace of technology and technical skills in digital humanities, resulting in an equally uncritical embrace of the postulates of techno-solutionism. "It allows us to believe that the problem facing our students and our profession is a lack of technical savvy rather than an economic system that undermines the future of our students" (ibid., p. 2)

The question about the role of digital humanities as the humanities' lifebelt on the sinking ship of academia introduces another point of debate, namely the issue of funding. As previously mentioned, Liu and other digital humanists gathered around the initiative *4Humanities* believe that digital humanities has a special potential to advocate for humanities in the broader academic and socioeconomic arena. Digital humanities "catch the eye of administrators and funding agencies who otherwise dismiss the humanities as yesterday's news," these scholars argue (see 4Humanities, Mission). Raley (2014) similarly situates digital humanities in the broader socioeconomic context of contemporary higher education, but, in a less favorable tone, excludes coincidental character of digital humanities emerging "at the same moment that the neoliberalization and corporatization of higher education has intensified" (p. 4). Hugget (2012), on the other hand, highlights a negative outlook on digital humanities held among some of the humanists, where this field is seen as "the monster that is garnering all the attention and sucking up available research funding" (p. 86).

Although this few has been fairly present in public debates of digital humanities, its grounding is questionable. As an example, the biggest US funding program for humanities, The National Endowment for the Humanities, allocated the smallest funding—3.7 percent of its overall budget—to digital humanities in the fiscal year 2013. The funding controversies around digital humanities are thus probably best resolved in Rhody's (2014) words: "Funding overall is scarce. Period. Humanists are not in competition with digital humanists for funding: humanists are in competition with everyone for more funding" (pp. 10–11).

From Digital Humanities to Digital Humanists

In an attempt to move beyond the debates and controversies in digital humanities, "what counts as digital humanities and what does not, who is in and who is out, and whether DH is about making or theorizing," Spiro (2012, p. 16) proposes that the digital humanities community should compile a comprehensive list of the guiding principles and values that it embraces, and then share this value statement with its members and with the public. Spiro argues that the digital humanities community bridges traditional humanistic values, such as critical thinking, debate, pluralism, exploration, and critique with values of the digital culture, including openness, transparency, and sharing. Drawing on the analysis of digital humanities manifestos, mission statements, and other documents, Spiro proposes an initial set of values that encapsulate the goals digital humanities community hopes to accomplish.

These values are "openness," which includes open access and open code, as well as the open exchange of ideas; "collaboration" where the community promotes an ethos of interdisciplinary collaboration, a penchant for new methods and epistemologies and fully acknowledges participants' contributions; "collegiality" and "connectedness," including a nonhierarchical ethos of mutual learning and excluding any "in group/out group" polarizations; "diversity" of scholarly and sociocultural richness because as Spiro notes, "the digital humanities community pays lip service to diversity but has not engaged with it on a deeper level" (p. 28); and "experimentation" as the primary method of exploration and knowledge production, where the community recognizes the value of play, innovation, and failure in the pursuit of innovation (ibid., p. 30).

Whether a shared value statement of digital humanities could be formulated, and, if so, whether it would bring about a coherent identity of the field remains to be seen. For now, unresolved disciplinary questions and debates create circumstances in which the descriptors progressively developing, diversifying, and intensifying can be applied equally to digital humanities as a field, and to the controversies that surround it. Under such circumstances, the approach that refocuses our analytical lens from digital *humanities* to digital *humanists* gains in prominence. Svensson (2010) postulates that another, and potentially more fruitful way, of discussing the highly contested field of digital humanities is by analyzing scholars' individual practices:

> It would seem tenable to state that minimally, digital humanities is manifested by a single scholar, teacher, artist, programmer, engineer or student doing some kind of work—thinking, reflecting, writing, creating—at the intersection of the humanities and information technology—or by "products" resulting from such activities. (para. 48)

Svensson warns that the term digital humanist might be too general to capture disciplinary differences, and simultaneously, too narrowly focused on the technical side of scholarly practice in digital humanities. On the other hand, he also notes that unlike the strategy-driven term digital humanities, the singular designator is increasingly becoming a spontaneous mode of scholars' self-identification (para. 51). Kirschenbaum (2014) concurs, offering that although we might never know what digital humanities is, it is certain that digital humanities will always be somebody's work. Based on this conclusion, he argues for the analysis of digital humanities in action.

This particular approach—the study of digital humanities in action and across several analytical levels, from individual to organizational—governed the ethnographic study that formed the empirical foundation of this book, and which is described in the following section.

An Ethnographic Look at Digital Humanities

As mentioned in the opening of this chapter, the ethnographer's epistemic studio encompasses complex and seemingly fuzzy social formations and practices articulated through accounts that Geertz (1973) has famously defined as "thick descriptions." What is sometimes misunderstood, however, is that thickness does not primarily refer to the ethnographic narrative, but to the associated intellectual effort of recognizing, connecting, and understanding the thickness of myriad elements constituting contextualized behavior. As Geertz explains,

> What the ethnographer is in fact faced with ... is a multiplicity of complex conceptual structures, many of them superimposed upon or knotted into one another, which are at once strange, irregular, and inexplicit, and which he must contrive somehow first to grasp and then to render. (p. 10)

This aspect of ethnographic work made it a widely accepted method for empirical investigations of scientific and scholarly practice, and for creating ethnographic accounts of the complexity of "science observed" (see Knorr-Cetina and Mulkay, 1983). Ethnographic studies involving scientific labs proliferated throughout the 1980s and 1990s, popularizing views of scholarly communities as "tribes" (Latour and Woolgar, 1979), science and epistemic cultures (Knorr Cetina, 1999), and established the importance of studying scholars in action (see Traweek, 1988; Latour, 1988; Pickering, 1992; Downey and Dumit, 1997; Forsythe, 2001).

Focus on epistemic cultures and disciplinary assumptions still constitutes a recognized framework for analyzing scholarly practice, including those in the digital humanities. For instance, one of the core questions Collins et al. (2012) pose in their examination of technology use in the humanities is how humanists' "learned behaviors, principles and habits respond to the computing-driven changes within the information environment" (p. 79). Likewise, Svensson (2012) proposes to understand digital humanities as a trading zone (see Galison, 1997) connecting disciplinary communities of practice. In the context of digital humanities projects, Dombrowski (2014) describes the planning phase of the Bamboo Project, which anticipated the main challenges to arise because "each [participating] community has distinctive practices, lingo, assumptions, and concerns" (p. 2).

Acknowledging relevance of disciplinary assumptions and habits also constituted an important element of this study, but it did so with a cautionary voice. This caution stems from recognition that recontextualization of analytical concepts, though inherent to knowledge production, has important epistemological consequences. When the concept of "culture" passes into

diverse discourses, it is commonly misconstrued as the conceptualization of "difference," seen presumably as a homogenous
set of values and behaviors (see Barth, 1995). This is a critical
point for studies of epistemic cultures, where such misconstrued
understanding of culture might lead to stereotypical differen-
tiations among scholarly communities on the one hand, and to
assumptions about alleged coherence within those communities on the other. To paraphrase Ingold (2002/1994), however,
what ethnographers of epistemic cultures "do *not* find are neatly
bounded and mutually exclusive bodies of thought and custom,
perfectly shared by all who subscribe to them, and in which their
lives and works are fully encapsulated" (p. 330; emphasis in the
original). Deliberations about scholarly work sometimes too easily mobilize presumed epistemic coherences and differences,
offering simplified explanations, such as those of humanists as
"lone scholars" who are shunning collaboration due to disciplinary habits. As I discuss in chapters 3 and 4, a plethora of epistemological and methodological aspects influence collaborative
research in the humanities, aside from presumed disciplinary
patterns. Even more importantly, forms of humanists' coopera-
tion do not necessarily fit formulaic models about what scholarly collaboration *is* or *should be*. Ethnographic accounts bring
forward such complexities, challenging assumptions of epistemic
cultural essentialism.

An additional peril of shallowly approaching the concept
of epistemic cultures is that epistemic identities adopted or
assigned on the basis of presumed disciplinary coherences open
the door to boundary work and to *in-group/out-out group* polar-
ization, corresponding to those still unfolding in the field of
digital humanities. Such approaches also "encourage the strategic construction of polarizing debates that translate into
battles of influence" (Op.cit., p. 62), as I discuss in chapter 5
with regard to digital knowledge production in the humanities. To overcome such debates, Barth proposes reversing the
overused notion of knowledge-as-culture to potentially more
rewarding culture-as-knowledge. Namely, conceptualizing culture as knowledge recognizes that culture, just like knowledge

production, comes about through the constant ebb and flow of practice, materialized as different ways of knowing within and among scholarly communities of practice:

> "Knowledge" is not characterizable as difference: indeed, the same or similar knowledge is obviously used and reproduced in different local populations to provide grounds for their thoughts and actions. But there are also very divergent bodies of knowledge and different ways of knowing within populations as well as between them. (Op.cit., p. 66)

Continuing this line of reasoning, ethnographic look at digital knowledge production in the humanities analyses an interaction of coexisting possibilities rather than projected differences, presuming a chance to always be surprised. As Strathern (2005) puts it, "the axiom that everything could always be otherwise," despite the analyst's theoretical inclinations and premises, is one of the axioms of ethnographic work. (p. 425). I conducted my ethnographic study among the digital humanists from an analogous starting perspective. I accepted that whichever assumptions about this area of humanities scholarship might exist, and whichever assumptions I might knowingly or unknowingly hold, in practice they could always be different. Yet, I did not approach digital knowledge production in practice as a binary counterpart or a corrective to digital knowledge production in theory. Instead, I approached it as heuristic, as a perspective for understanding theory *and* practice as mutually constitutive spheres of digital knowledge production in the humanities.

The ethnographic study was conducted from 2010 to 2013 as part of the research projects described in the "Introduction" chapter. Through case studies, surveys, in-depth interviews, and observations, the study sought to highlight issues relevant to understanding how scholarly practices codevelop with digital technologies, particularly in the humanities. I explored how scholars engage with and think about digital tools, methods, and resources; I interviewed teams developing digital research tools and observed digital resource use within academic research units.

The fieldwork was carried out at 23 educational, research, and funding institutions in the United States and Europe. It involved 258 participants including researchers, faculty, students, university administrators, librarians, software developers, policy makers, and funders.

The study comprised two phases. The first phase focused on digital scholarship in the humanities, exploring the situatedness of digital tools, methods, and resources in everyday scholarly practice, challenges of research tool development, criteria for funding and evaluating digital research projects, approaches to establishing research centers and educational initiatives, and so on. Participants consulted in this research phase worked in different roles, disciplines, institutions, and countries, which afforded an opportunity to compare a range of strategies and directions in contemporary digital humanities.

Figure 1.2   Smiljana Antonijević interviewing a respondent.

The second phase employed a different comparative perspective; namely, a multidisciplinary perspective of exploring how scholars across disciplines, including sciences, social sciences, and humanities engage with digital technologies in their work. This research phase also analyzed minute details of scholarly workflow, examining how digital research tools and methods get integrated at different stages of the research cycle. The focus was on understanding humanists' engagement with digital technologies, but contextualizing this focus within an interdisciplinary framework was critical for understanding the specifics of digital humanities as part of digital scholarship.

The results of these two phases of the ethnographic study form the empirical basis for inquiry into the changing landscape of humanities scholarship presented in the following chapters. Chapter 2 considers transformations in scholarly practice from the perspective of individual scholars, chapter 3 looks at the transformations of humanities disciplines, while chapter 4 analyzes transformations in scholarly practice at the organizational level. The study thus employs a multi-scale inquiry into the processes of transformation in humanities scholarship. As Misa (2009) points out, "our findings about technology follow from the framings of our inquiries," and multi-scale inquiries help bridge the gap arising from such different framings (p. 359). This study juxtaposes transformations identified at the individual, disciplinary, and organizational levels, charting the areas of confluence and divergence among these three instances of academic practice.

This analytical component presumes establishing and sorting structures of significance. However, it also assumes a detailed record of practices in digital knowledge production observed close to the field. In the chapters that follow, I quote numerous study participants in hope that voices from the field will inspire dialogue among this book's audience. This approach sometimes muddies the ethnographic description, but, as Law (2004) points out, "simple clear descriptions don't work out if what they are describing is not itself very coherent. The very attempt to be clear simply increases the mess" (p. 2). The field of digital humanities, as both the discursive formation and practice, is far from coherent, and ethnographic look helps us uncover connections within this relative messiness of the field. Let us thus dig into ethnographic data of digital knowledge production in the humanities, hoping that this exploration will generate new connections, in addition to new answers.

CHAPTER 2

Workflows of Digital Scholars*

Observing technology-related changes in scholarly practice from the perspective of an individual scholar affords insights into the nuances and daily challenges of digital scholarly work. Although scholars commonly belong to formal or informal communities of practice that influence their research, the choices concerning the implementation of disciplinary or institutionally established uses of technology occur on an individual level. This initial empirical chapter of the present book thus compares, contrasts, and analyzes how individual scholars integrate digital technologies into their research workflows, exploring the ways in which transformations in digital scholarship occur from a bottom-up perspective.

In order to describe and analytically break down complexity of these workflows, I developed the following model (see figure 2.1)[1] to represent the general process as well as the following activities: collecting, finding, organizing, and analyzing research data and materials; writing up, annotating, and citing research data and materials; reflecting upon, sharing, communicating, and archiving research data and materials. The research activities presented in the model were not intended to be either comprehensive or mutually exclusive, but rather to serve as a heuristic for understanding the complexity of scholarly research process.

The diagram also served as a visual prompt in my fieldwork. As explained in chapter 1, I carried out an ethnographic study

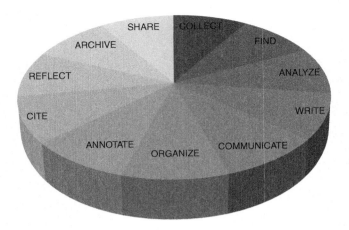

Figure 2.1 Research workflow.

between 2010–2013 at 23 educational, research and funding institutions in the United States and Europe, with 258 study participants. Through observations and in-depth interviews, the research focused on the minute details of scholarly workflow, examining how scholars integrate digital research tools and methods at different stages of the research cycle. Although the study focused on understanding humanists' engagement with digital technologies, it employed a comparative, multidisciplinary perspective to analyze how scholars across disciplines—including sciences, social sciences, and humanities —incorporate digital technologies into their work. This multidisciplinary approach was important for understanding the specifics of humanists' digital workflow as part of digital scholarship.

I began each interview asking the respondents which digital tools[2] they use in their research. Following the response, I showed each respondent my Research Workflow diagram (figure 2.1) and asked the respondent to use the chart to guide me through specifics of his or her digital technology use in each of the phases shown in the diagram. Commonly, respondents would then list a set of digital tools not mentioned in the previous answer, explaining that they had forgotten about a particular research activity and a corresponding tool.

Figure 2.2 An interviewee explaining his workflow using the Research Workflow diagram.

The use of the visual prompt enabled me thus to develop a more detailed overview of the variety of digital tools scholars use in their research practices, and to understand the influence these tools have on segments of scholarly practice that become routinized and thus invisible to analytic inquiry. Knowledge in practice can be hard to articulate or recall, so it is important to study it through the goals scholars seek to achieve in those activities (see Carlile, 2002).

The results of the investigation showed that digital tools and resources have different roles and levels of integration at various phases of the scholarly workflow. Accordingly, the perceived and/or actual influence of these tools differed across individual segments of the workflow as well as across academic disciplines. Yet, in certain phases of the workflow the use of digital tools and resources was prevalent irrespective of individual or disciplinary preferences. These phases of the workflow included finding research data and materials, writing, and communicating. In these activities, digital tools are used daily and systematically, regardless of a scholar's academic background or level of technical proficiency. These activities are thus similar to Unsworth's (2000) concept of "scholarly primitives," as well as McCarty and Short's (2002) notion of "methodological commons." Generally, these are the elements of scholars' initial uptake of digital technologies into research practice and the areas where they perceive the impact of digital tools on their research as most extensive. I start by discussing the first of these activities where digital tools and resource are used across disciplines, the activity of finding research data and materials. I then continued along the segments of digital scholarly workflow named in figure 2.1.

Finding Research Data and Materials

Finding and accessing research data and materials electronically is a standard, daily practice of respondents consulted in this study. They considered this activity one of the most important benefits of incorporating digital technologies into their research practice. This is particularly noticeable among the humanities scholars, for whom electronic access to research materials represents one of the key transformations in research practice. "To me, online bibliographies have been the major, major, major tool that has completely changed the possibilities for research projects," said an associate professor of French. She explained that for her first book, published 20 years ago, she had to collect all the information by hand, on a remote research site. She thus finds electronic search and access "the single most helpful thing," which has been of critical importance for her work.

Scholars in the sciences and social sciences also identified the transformative role of electronic search on their research practices. For instance, a professor of astrophysics related that he rarely goes to the library now that he can search the catalogs online, as well as read and conduct research from his office. He pointed out, however, that digital technologies offer more than mere conveniences, as he now has access to preprints as well as the ability to distribute his work before publication. "The ability to get things from people, to distribute things, to search for things made a tremendous impact on my work," he concluded. Another respondent, an associate professor of political sciences whose research focuses on developing countries, acknowledged that electronic access to sources has significantly improved her workflow and overall research: "Being able to quickly, within seconds, access newspapers from Indonesia, for example, helps me a lot."

Diverse information sources serve as search and access points, including academic and commercial collections, disciplinary databases, Web search engines, as well as scholars' personal digital libraries and other individually created resources. Across disciplines, the path toward finding information online commonly starts with Google Search and Google Scholar. These search engines are especially popular with scholars engaged in discovery search.[3] Google Search and Google Scholar are also preferred when scholars seek to identify different connective structures, such as citations or specialized indexing vocabularies based on associative thinking and collective associative thinking, as envisioned by Bush (1945) and Garfield (1955), respectively.

Library databases, by comparison, are the more typical access points for humanities scholars, especially if they are engaged in confirmation search, that is, a known item search. Increasingly, however, the respondents' information-seeking behavior favors commercial services, which are perceived as faster and more precise than academic search engines. As an associate professor of English explained, "Sometimes the [library] database just doesn't pick up things or you have to go to multiple databases, so then you're going back and forth, and that's not fun." Researchers also preferred commercial services for their sophisticated search functionality, which enabled them to move toward more advanced text mining. One respondent, a PhD student of comparative literature, explained that his latest project centered on a very long poem he analyzed for specific variations and word combinations: "So, I use Google Books for that. Even though I have a copy of the book myself, it's quicker than searching through it physically."

These findings reassert the results of previous studies on scholars' information-seeking behavior, which have already prompted academic libraries to provide online search experience comparable to that of using Google[4] (see Nicholas et al., 2011; Asher et al., 2013). In this study, the advantages of commercial over academic research tools and services were also identified in other segments of digital workflow, which suggests that academic tools and services must better address user needs in order to compete with commercial services. One possible path toward that improvement is establishing better collaboration between tool users and tool developers, as I discuss further in chapters 4 and 5.

Scholars' personal digital collections also function as an important information resource. They provide quick access to research materials and transform scholars' work through increased mobility and flexibility:

> Research is much more portable; I can bring my entire library's worth of video to Starbucks and be working on it. I don't have to be in the darkroom with the editing board at a certain place at a certain time. So, I've been able to really do my work anywhere. (Associate professor of education)

Reasserting the role of digital tools as cognitive artifacts (see Norman, 1993; Brey, 2005), respondents in my study noted that increased portability of research materials influences their cognitive functioning by creating a "mobile memory," which constantly moves with them, and which researchers consider to be more efficient and accurate than when they rely on memorized information.

A specific type of information search is related to the use of digital information aggregators, that is, local and web-based applications that tap multiple sources of data. While humanities and social sciences scholars rarely used aggregators, scholars in the sciences did so extensively to stay abreast of developments and news in their fields. For instance, one professor of chemistry accesses aggregators on a daily basis to gain important disciplinary updates. The aggregator he consults compiles information from the American Chemical Society, the Royal Chemical Society, and similar professional organizations to distribute the latest abstracts on a continuous basis. The respondent explains that by the evening hours everything for the day has been published, and the aggregator allows him to search those materials to check for information most relevant to his work.

Although the respondents overwhelmingly accept electronic search and access tools, they also voiced some caution. Similar to Brabazon (2007), an assistant professor of design remarked that the new generation of *"I Want It Now"* scholars, as she dubs them, suffers from a search bias. They rely heavily on contemporary search sources, some of which could overlook older, foundational bodies of scholarship. "Because the information is so easy to find, they just do surface level skimming and just reuse that content and say, 'That's good enough'" Such information-seeking behavior becomes especially important when considered relative to the increasing prevalence of Google Scholar and Google Search, whose built-in content limitations and search biases have been repeatedly identified, despite certain recent improvements (see Jasco, 2005; Neuhaus et al., 2005; de Winter et al., 2014).

Citing

Referencing research data and materials in future work comprises an indispensable part of scholarly workflow. Digital citation management tools can relieve scholars from the arduous task of manually typing and reformatting citations. Despite this apparent benefit of automating the citation process, my study revealed a relatively low use of citation managers across disciplines.

While academics actively use digital tools to find research materials, they rely less frequently on those tools for creating bibliographic citations. This finding might be surprising given that digital citation management has been part of university services and library training programs for years; the majority of respondents in this study indicated that they learned about citation management programs early in their careers, usually at graduate school. This implies that although institutional support and training programs increase uptake of digital tools, these factors are insufficient for effectively integrating tools into scholarly practice.

Respondents in the humanities and social sciences reported dissatisfaction with the existing citation managers as a common reason for bypassing those tools. The respondents pointed out that even though they took classes or tested citation managers such as *EndNote*, *Zotero*, or *Mendeley*, "all of those had issues" that made it easier for them to continue manually managing citations. Yet, most of the respondents believe that those tools would be beneficial for their work:

> It is unbelievable that I don't use any of those [citation managers]. I still have my graduate assistant help me to draft my bibliographies. I can see that I would develop my bibliographies so much easily and quicker. (Assistant professor of media studies)

Scholars in the humanities and social sciences who did report using citation managers most commonly chose *EndNote*. Usually, they adopted this program as graduate students and continued working with it in their academic careers, despite a general level of dissatisfaction:

> Am I satisfied with it [*EndNote*]? Not really. It's not very intuitive. Why I use it? I guess when I was in graduate school somebody recommended it to me and I just bought it. (Assistant professor of English as a second language)

A tendency among scholars in the humanities and social sciences to keep using certain digital research tools despite dissatisfaction existed in other segments of their workflow, too. This finding confirms persistence of certain disciplinary habits recognized in earlier studies (e.g., Nicholas et al., 2009; Tenopir et al., 2004), but it also indicates the lack of humanists' influence on the development of digital research tools, as I discuss in chapter 4.

Among interviewees in the sciences, the most commonly used citation managers are *BibTex* and *Papers*. The use of *BibTex* is a logical continuation of the science scholars' intensive use of *LaTex* document preparation program for writing, discussed later in this chapter, as *BibTex* comes bundled with *LaTex*. As an assistant professor of biology explained, "I write all of my articles in [La]*TeX*, so *BibTeX* is a natural format, and there's a couple tools that relate to that."

Scholars in the sciences also tend to use more than one citation manager, combining them according to how the software best fits their research workflow. As a case in point, a professor of astrophysics explained that he uses *BibTeX* when writing, because it integrates well with *LaTeX*, but switches to *Papers* when communicating with colleagues:

> I'll be responding in an e-mail to someone and I'll say, "You really need to look at this, or have you seen that," and I can basically just drag the reference and it will come out in Harvard form or something like that, so, for that purpose *Papers* is very, very useful. The difficulty is that it means that I have my library in two different places.

These disciplinary differences observed in scholars' use of citation managers transform into significant distinctions when we examine how scholars collect and analyze their research data and materials, which is the topic of the next section.

Collecting and Analyzing

When discussing data collection and analysis practices, interviewees in the sciences commonly noted that their work would be impossible without digital tools and resources. "Half of the work that's done in the lab generates electronic data, and that's all based off of instruments that are run by computers, the data they gather," says an assistant professor of chemistry, while his senior colleague, an associate professor of chemistry, adds "everything is computer-based, without it we wouldn't be able to do any of the research, we just couldn't do it, period." For these scholars, data collection and analysis have become unachievable without digital tools and methods, which is one end of the complexity continuum in digital scholarship. Yet, as I discuss further in chapter 5, digital scholarship spans a wide complexity spectrum, and should be broadly conceived as scholarly activities that prompt changes in the ways researchers envision, carry out, communicate, and organize their work and approach their objects of inquiry. This is particularly relevant in the humanities, where artificial boundaries between "digital" and "mainstream" scholarship obscure the fact that the work of contemporary humanists would be fundamentally different, if not impossible, without digital technologies.

The importance of understanding digital scholarship across the complexity spectrum equally pertains to the science disciplines. A variety of epistemological and methodological specificities influence disciplinary and individual research practices, so assuming homogeneity in the role and impact of digital tools across the sciences is misleading. In this study, a number of science scholars reported combining digital and analog data collection and analyses practices, although digital tools and methods increasingly take prominence. A professor of kinesiology explained, for instance, that she measures physical activity in the field by using both "pen and pencil" methods, as well as digital tools such as accelerometers and pedometers, because their analytical software facilitates her research process.

Among the respondents in the social sciences, digital research tools and methods have steadily developed into a "new methodological normal" ever since the 1990s. Digital tools and methods, including online surveys, Skype interviewing, digital audio and video recording, smartphones, and netbooks have all assumed a regular role in data collection and analysis practices:

> My major project is in South Africa, and we collect data through netbooks; we had about 10,000 students in that sample. We also observe teachers teaching the lessons, and we use digitally-recorded video and audio-recordings of the teachers. Prior to that, we had about 7,000 students and we collected data using smartphones. All of that, data collection, questions, ability to share is a benefit to my research. (Professor of youth development and public policy)

This interviewee explained that all the data used in her study is collected in South Africa, and then sent electronically to her research facility in the United States, where an interdisciplinary team examines large amounts of longitudinal data in multiple ways at multiple times.

In addition to enabling international and interdisciplinary collaboration, integration of digital tools also facilitates data analysis in social science research. For instance, an associate professor of sociology observed that video analysis proved a difficult analytic process prior to the introduction of digital research tools: "Now there are programs that live on your laptop that allow you to just touch a button and code your video, so it's made my job as a researcher pretty easy," she noted.

While useful for data collection, digital tools and methods were reported as less effective for data analysis. As a case in point, an assistant professor of education said that he uses *Qualtrics* for online surveys, as well as digital video to collect his research data, but he does not use digital tools to analyze that data:

> I don't use something like SPSS or NVivo to crunch that data, principally because the type of analysis that I'm doing is interpretive, so it doesn't lend itself to accounting scheme per se.

Similarly, an assistant professor of gender studies acknowledged that digital technologies influence the way she thinks about collecting data and developing relationships with research participants, but do not change her data analysis process: "I'm an interpretivist, so I use ethnographic methods, and I don't crunch numbers at all," she explains.

Indeed, both social scientists and humanists sometimes equate digital methods with "data crunching," arguing that "going digital" and "staying qualitative" are incongruent routes (see Brown, 2002). One pole of this argument holds that meaning cannot be "arrived at algorithmically," perceiving digital research tools and methods as a challenge to traditional hermeneutics. The alternative view posits that algorithmic complexity does not imply reducing analysis to a discussion of numbers; rather, it presumes that digital research tools and methods can support interpretative analysis, particularly with increased methodological transparency and with digital tools recast as to support ambiguity and uncertainty of interpretative work (see Zenil, 2011; Gibbs and Owens, 2012).

A significant number of humanists who participated in my study said they did not use digital tools and methods for data analysis. Lack of digital technologies in humanists' analytical practice sometimes stems from previously mentioned skepticism toward "algorithmically reached" interpretation. An associate professor of French observed, for instance, that while digital technologies might enable new aspects of research to arise, "the old-fashioned work of thinking and reading has not changed." In contrast, an assistant professor of Spanish posited that the use of digital tools and methods could facilitate her analytical process:

> No [I do not use digital tools], and I should. I'm looking at literary texts for the current manuscript project that were created by a range of authors from the 1940s on to the present. . . . And indeed, there would be a kind of lexical search that would be very handy. I'm sure I'm losing valuable time in that respect, but I don't know how to do that yet.

Similarly, a professor of musicology shared how using digital tools and methods recently helped his analysis achieve a breakthrough finding and inspired him to set up his own database for scholars working on literary and musical Renaissance madrigals. Specifying that he has a very rich, indexed data corpus he would like to share, he acknowledged that his lack of technical savvy prevents him from doing so: "Here I am, seventy years old, and like many humanists of my age, I'm not used to this kind of thing."

Indeed, most of the humanities respondents identified the lack of instruction and learning opportunities as a central barrier to adopting digital tools and methods in their analytical practices. A frequent failure of humanities departments to recognize digital literacy as an essential competence of contemporary scholars impedes researchers in developing those skills as part of their professional development program and paid time. Instead, they invest their free time, and, when needed, their own funding, which additionally undermines their enthusiasm for digital scholarship. The insufficiency of institutional support also limits scholars in discovering and using the full range of digital research tools and methods. For instance, my respondents often use a specific tool because their institution supports it technically and/or financially, rather than because it is the tool best suited to their research needs.

Younger humanities scholars use digital tools and methods for data analysis more prominently than their senior peers. For instance, an assistant professor of comparative literature explained that his latest book was based on an extensive electronic database he created and analyzed with the help of a statistician: "All that was computerized and digitized, and I worked with a statistician, who then did some of the math that I didn't have the ability to do. That's something that would not have been possible without the aid of the technology," this respondent concludes.

In archeology, digital technologies such as GIS applications, laser scanning, or databases have been used for decades, and they are as common as a trowel or any other archeological tool. There is no real distinction between digital and non-digital tools in the work of archeologists, explains an assistant professor of archeology, and describes the advantages of digital technology in his research:

With one of the 3D modeling projects, I've used sunlight simulation scripts, which allowed me to look at the particular lighting situation of a house in Pompeii at a particular moment in time. If you recontextualized the mosaics by putting them back into their original environment of a reconstructed house and then simulate the sunlight, you can better experience how the ancients, themselves, witnessed the art.

Similarly, another interviewee reflects on her project on tracing the transmission of segments of knowledge about the alphabet, and explicates the specific epistemological benefits digital methods bring to her work:

Creating that genealogical tree and history of textual transmission is easier to do in a digital environment.... You can create webs of connection and relations among objects where the webs themselves call those objects back into play, rather than simply having them being affixed sequence in organization. (Professor of bibliographical studies)

The analytical work on her project would be challenging, if not impossible, without the use of digital tools and methods, she emphasized. These examples suggest that employing digital tools and methods in humanists' analytical work can play a very significant role, although it might still be outside the disciplinary mainstream practices. Humanists' lower uptake of digital technologies in analytical work is a multifaceted subject and is discussed further in chapters 4 and 5.

Organizing and Storing

The part of scholarly workflow closely related to data collection and analysis is organizing those materials in useful and reliable ways and storing them for further use.[5] In the sciences, respondents clearly distinguish between storing and organizing research articles and research data. The former constitutes less of a challenge, and it is often accomplished through the use of citation management tools, such as *Papers* and *JabRef*:

> When I've identified things that are useful, it [*Papers*] has a bunch of Smart Folders. I make sure everything I read I give some sort of rating, and that's how I keep track of what I've read. That's by and large how I handle almost everything. (Professor of biology)

Organizing and storing research data, by contrast, posed one of the greatest challenges to respondents in the sciences, whose work routinely generates vast amounts of data that need to be available on a daily basis: "A real issue, in terms of storage, is the ability to bring over and manage large data sets where I need to work intensively on them. It is just not there," complained a professor of astrophysics. Furthermore, since data sharing is "religiously accepted" in the sciences, as my respondents put it, they also struggle to organize stored materials in a way that supports data sharing and reuse:

> It's one thing to say that I have it [data] and I can make it available to you, but is it organized? I could certainly give my dataset to anybody, but without me there answering their question 24/7, it is

useless to them. It is the documentation, organization, reliability, the metadata that make that information not simply useful, but usable in any way, shape or form. (Professor of physics)

The issue of data management becomes especially important with recent requirements from major funding agencies that applicants submit their data management plans for each of the proposed projects (see Asher et al., 2013). Respondents in my study support such initiatives, but express concern that neither funders nor academic institutions provide scholars with the financial, technical, or legal support necessary to manage increasingly complex data. Among respondents in the humanities and social sciences, cloud-based services, particularly Dropbox, are popular for storing and organizing research materials:

I use Dropbox for everything. It has saved my life, it has changed my life. I paid for a larger Dropbox storage, but because I travel so much, it is the best thing ever. It [research materials] is all Dropbox synchronized, and it's organized well enough for me to find stuff. (Professor of sociology)

Another respondent, a professor of youth development, echoed this sentiment, stressing that she travels internationally a lot, and having Dropbox on her laptop and cellphone enables her to access her research materials at any time and any place. Again, increased mobility of both scholars and their research materials is seen as one of the most significant benefits of implementing digital tools in research practice.

Some scholars, however, distrust commercial cloud-based services, such as Dropbox, citing concerns about privacy and long-term sustainability. An assistant professor of education criticized cloud services for their poor privacy systems, saying that he uses cloud service sharing only for nonconfidential materials.

In some cases, institutional concerns about data privacy prohibit scholars from using commercial services, despite their potential technical advantages. An associate professor of psychology reported that privacy issues and IRB requirements obligated her team to use university storage services instead of commercial providers, even though those services created storage and organization problems for her team:

> Right now we're using ANGEL [the University software platform] because it's a secure site, so it will meet the IRB [requirements]. But it's just really awkward. It won't hold the big videos. There's no revision capacity within a file. Can't organize any of the videos there. That's a real problem. Unfortunately, with secure data, we cannot put things like that on Dropbox.[6]

The extent to which privacy issues influence storing practices can best be observed in the case of scholars whose work requires such a high level of security that neither commercial nor institutional cloud-based services prove sufficiently reliable. For instance, an associate professor of education says that her research data are stored on a password-protected hard drive kept under lock and key in her filing cabinet:

> Really, the biggest thing is security. If it wasn't completely secure, it couldn't be used. I don't actually know of anybody working with footage of elementary school students that doesn't use the lock and key method.

Data storage and management remains a serious problem across disciplines, but with distinctive disciplinary needs. While storage capacity emerges as a challenge in the sciences, high security and privacy requirements characterize needs in the social sciences. The technical architecture of digital research tools thus needs to support specific disciplinary needs in ways that address disciplinary differences.

In addition to security issues, lack of technical skills also prevents some scholars in the humanities and social sciences from relying upon cloud-based services. Instead, they use flash drives, hard drives, or hard copy to store and organize their research materials. A professor of linguistics shared that she stores research materials on computer hard drives, and further manages them in the following way:

> I have three computers and a USB key, which is my little, precious, precious tool. It's very complicated because when I work

in one place, I have to make sure that the latest version of what I've done is transferred to each machine in due time. I do have all the versions of it on paper, as well. It's kind of an old-fashioned security thing.

Old-fashioned storing practices often go hand-in-hand with old-fashioned organizing practices, neither of which works effectively for electronic materials. An associate professor of English clarified:

> I used to be better at organizing, and it became this volume of stuff. And I had a complete breakdown of my organization system. In my past, not so long ago past, it was those paper copies that were really my source, my organization. It was open, the file drawer, and here's all the materials used for some particular study. Things are now online. And that's really where I need to clean up and adjust my old organization system.

This response also illustrates how integration of digital tools in one phase of the research process influences other segments of the workflow. Specifically, scholars' reorientation on electronic search and access produces an abundance of collected materials, requiring adjustments in researchers' storing and organizing practices, developed for print-based materials. So, while implementing digital tools into one phase of the workflow might be rewarding, it could also present a challenge in other phases of the work. Digital research tools should thus be designed to support a continuous research workflow, enabling scholars to navigate among separate, yet interconnected activities.

Writing

While storing and organizing research data and materials might still in some instances be related to hard copy paper forms, writing, however, is one of the workflow phases that has migrated completely to the digital realm. This is true across all disciplinary and generational categories examined in this study. In various disciplines, differences were observed with regard to the specific digital tools used and the extent of collaborative writing, but reliance on digital writing tools was a conclusive finding.

Among respondents in the humanities and social sciences, Microsoft *Word* is the primary tool used for both individual and collaborative writing. Writing is one of the scholarly activities where digital technologies were first incorporated into respondents' work and used pervasively since. Remembering early in her research career when she worked on an Olympia typewriter, a professor of Dutch praised *Word* processing as "a massive improvement over everything." A professor of musicology recollected his similar introduction to digital writing technologies:

> In my field of study, first of all there was the use of Word processing, which has been going on for 25 years now, and it made a tremendous difference to your ability to actually correct, and so you didn't have to use carbon paper to take it to the typist.

Yet, changes in scholarly writing brought by digital tools are not always regarded as fully positive. An assistant professor of Japanese explains that writing involves two basic skills, recognition and production; digital character input has categorically changed the production aspect of writing in Japanese, for both native and non-native speakers, who have lost their production skills:

> You talk to a person and you say, "OK, write that character down." They whip out their cell phone, type it on the cell phone, and that character pops up; they can recognize it, but they can't actually produce it with their hand. This is a way in which the technology has deeply affected our cognitive way of dealing with written language. That's a real change that the technology has caused and one that feels like a step backwards.

A recent Pew report found similar concerns. A majority of teachers surveyed in the report responded that, due to the prevalence of digital tools, students are more prone to taking shortcuts, put less effort into their writing, and are more careless with grammar (see Purcell et al., 2013).

When using Word in collaborative writing, scholars in the humanities and social sciences rely on Track Changes functionality, and then exchange edited versions with collaborators via Dropbox or e-mail. Although aware of platforms for collaborative writing, such as Google Docs, most respondents in the humanities and social sciences prefer to exchange Word documents via Dropbox. They see the advantage of such an approach in integrating writing with research materials stored at Dropbox, so that everything they need for a project is at one place.

Scholars in the humanities and social sciences are aware that such a way of working was not designed for collaborative writing and thus has various challenges, which they attempt to solve in different ways. Sometimes, the problem of versioning gets resolved by adding a collaborator's initials to the end of the document, thus marking a version that should further be used by other collaborators.

But this kind of practice is changing with younger scholars. For them, collaborative writing platforms become so vital, that they shape the epistemological and methodological character of their research. An assistant professor of comparative literature describes his book translation project with a colleague abroad in which the use of Google Docs made an important epistemological difference. "We started off in a kind of standard way," he says. He and his collaborator each chose chapters to translate and then uploaded the translations to Google Docs. Next, they each edited the other's work. Finally, they returned the new, edited version to the original author for one more revision. "It came to the point where now, somebody shows me a sentence and the translation and I don't know if I was the original translator of it or him," this scholar stresses, adding that in his view the final translations benefitted from such way of working. "I could go and find out exactly who did what because the documents have a history, but I prefer not to. That's one project I can point to where absolutely it would have been different [without technology]," he concludes.

In the sciences, digital tools are equally indispensable to both individual and collaborative writing. However, the tools science scholars choose differ from those used by their colleagues in the humanities and social sciences. Among the respondents in the sciences, LaTex document preparation system and document markup language is a dominant writing tool. "All my writing is in LaTeX," says a professor of physics; "We usually write all papers using LaTex," corroborates an assistant professor of chemistry;

"I write all of my articles in LaTeX," agrees a professor of biology, and so on. LaTex is often used as the underlying writing system, supplemented with the use of text editing programs such as *Sublime Text* or *WinEdt*.

Respondents in the science remembered circulating collaborative documents via e-mail before switching to versioning tools designed to support coauthorship. Subversion control system is the most widely used program. For instance, a professor of astrophysics explained that Subversion allows him and his collaborators to work simultaneously on a document without colliding or affecting each other's work. An assistant professor of mathematics similarly stated that he prefers *Subversion* for collaborative writing, but cautioned that this program requires a high level of technical proficiency and thus is best used when all collaborators have the same skill level.

Annotating and Reflecting

A specific type of writing includes annotating research materials and writing up research reflections. An inquiry into annotation practices of respondents in this study shows a variety of styles and preferences both across academic disciplines and in terms of individual inclinations.

A number of respondents in the humanities and social sciences reported avoiding digital annotation tools, stressing that handwriting is their preferred method of annotation. Sometimes, the reason for that is the perception that none of the existing tools for digital annotation meets their research needs. A professor of rhetoric, for example, explained that what struck him when he first began using computers in the 1970s was the need for a good digital note-taking system. To this day, he has not found one. For other respondents, the lack of technical savvy is the main barrier to using digital annotation. An associate professor of history described her annotation practices in the following manner: "I am a dinosaur. Everybody at the library has their laptop and they go 'click, click, click.' I have reams of paper and lots of pencils."

However, the majority of respondents in the humanities and social sciences do use digital annotations, applying different note-taking techniques. Some of them type their comments in separate *Word* files rather than writing them in margins. The main reason for this seems to be the lack of knowledge about electronic annotation possibilities. For instance, a professor of comparative literature said she has yet to find a way to highlight text and make annotations in PDF files, so she types her comments in a *Word* file while reading, and then keeps that document together with the PDF file. "Certainly, searchable PDF's and annotatable PDF's would be very helpful," this respondent concludes, indicating that she is indeed unaware of PDFs being both searchable and annotatable. Similar experience describes a professor of linguistics, who explained that she creates a *Word* file to record her comments about whatever document she is reading, then e-mails the *Word* file to colleagues. "Only in the last year, when I've exchanged a document with one of my colleagues, I noticed that she had annotations in the margins. And I said, 'How do you do that?' So, I'm still just learning it," this interviewee explains.

In contrast to this, younger scholars do tend to write in-text annotations. For example, an assistant professor of education responded that he asks his students and collaborators to provide him with PDF files only, explaining it in the following way:

> What that allows me to do is download the collection of papers that people produce, open them and annotate them on my iPad with one of several different PDF annotation tools, or annotate them on my desktop with Preview, which is another important tool in my workflow, in terms of writing and editing and providing feedback.

These differences between how junior and senior scholars annotate their work confirms an observation offered by an associate director of Strategic Initiatives and Proposal Development. When I interviewed her about her collaborative experiences writing grant proposals, she noted:

> I find that the more senior faculty, rather than commenting within the grant document, will open a separate Word document and write up their comments. Younger faculty find it more time efficient to just type in the document and do those kinds of edits.

Finally, some of the respondents see the potential of digital technologies to transform annotation, as a traditional humanities practice into a contemporary method of collaborative reading and knowledge production. This is illustrated in the work of a professor of philosophy, who plans to invite the audience of his enhanced digital book to publish their annotations of his work online. In doing so, he hopes to maintain an ongoing dialogue and collaborative reading of the entire publication. "And the book actually argues for the importance of collaborative reading, through talking about how Plato's writing encourages us to read in an active way. So, it's bound up with the argument of the book," this scholar explains.

In line with such calls for active reading and collaboration are the annotation practices of respondents in the sciences, who commonly use digital annotations in their work. A number of these interviewees indicated using citation management programs for annotating materials. For instance, an assistant professor of chemistry explains that he almost exclusively uses *Papers* citation manager for annotations, describing it in the following way:

> I can mark them [documents] up either in here [on laptop] or on this iPad. It syncs between what I've done here and then what I have on iPad. Essentially, I can mark it up, highlight things, make notes and these notes appear back on the papers over there. It's pretty nice.

Interviewees in the sciences reported using these digital techniques in tandem with traditional annotation methods. A professor of statistics explained that he reads and annotates electronically, but when he wants to record more detail he prints out the materials and handwrites his notes. Likewise, an associate professor of genetics noted:" When I review articles, I annotate, but I do that on paper and then I copy it back to my reviews, so that's not really electronic, it's all done by hand."

A similar fusion of digital and "pen and paper" practices can also be found in the work phase of reflecting. Commonly, interviewees across disciplines describe reflecting as part of a research process that precedes writing and helps them organize their

Figure 2.3 A fusion of digital and "pen and paper" practices.

thoughts. The use or nonuse of digital tools during this phase appeared idiosyncratic, that is, based on scholars' personal preferences rather than disciplinary orientations.

In the humanities and social sciences, handwriting is often the first step of reflexive writing, followed by the use of digital tools. An associate professor of political science said that she captures her initial thoughts or notes by using pen and paper; once an organization for the paper emerges to her, she shifts to a Word file for writing phase. Yet, a number of respondents indicated that they reflect using only digital tools. "I use *Evernote* a lot for notes, and I've also been using *Scrivener* a little bit more for reflecting and getting ready to write, organizing things," explained a professor of philosophy. Similarly, an assistant professor of media studies said that she started using *Penzu* online diary program for writing her research notes and reflections once she got tired of carrying around her paper notebooks. Now, she has several *Penzu* diaries, one with reflections for the books she is writing, another for her forthcoming research project, and so on. In addition to portability, this respondent emphasized that *Penzu* facilitates her work by providing easy tagging, archiving, sharing, organizing, and similar functionalities, as well as accurately time-stamping entries for easy retrieval.

In the sciences, most of the respondents use digital tools to reflect on their work. A professor of astrophysics explained that he makes extensive use of Mind Mapping software, particularly when he is trying to organize his thinking:

> It's a very important way of organizing my thinking about different things, organizing papers before I start to write them and just reflecting and taking notes on things at meetings, I will typically have a Mind Map open. I would say that that has made a significant improvement in my ability to work efficiently and effectively and to think about things.

An assistant professor of engineering confessed to writing sticky notes about anything she is reflecting upon or trying to remember. She described her personal method for reflecting on electronic communications. "Even if I responded to the e-mail, I'll mark it as unread in my inbox so that I know to go back and look at it again. That's kind of my tool to go back and reflect on that e-mail and think about it more," she explained.

Finally, although digital tools for reflecting are generally popular among the scientists I interviewed, there were also scholars who preferred other methods. An assistant professor of mathematics explained, for instance, that he handwrites his rough notes on paper, and added: "I'll also write [my reflections] on the board and stare at it and hope that maybe a bolt of lightning strikes."

Communicating

Similar to the activity of reflecting, which tends to be influenced by individual rather than disciplinary differences, communicating is equally personal and disciplinary neutral. Of all the phases along the spectrum of a research workflow illustrated in my workflow diagram (figure 2.1), communicating is the only one where there were no observable differences along disciplinary lines. Similar to writing, communicating is fully intertwined with digital technologies, regardless of a scholar's disciplinary background or level of technical proficiency. Unlike writing, though, where scholarly fields differed in the type of digital writing tools they preferred, respondents from diverse fields identified the same digital tools they use for communicating.

Across all the disciplines, e-mail is a killer app. It is favored as less transient than other forms of communication, insomuch that it provides a written trail and an archive of exchanged messages, which a person can revisit at a later point. An additional benefit of e-mail is seen in its ability to integrate well with other tasks and tools. "I use Gmail for everything. Google Hangout is right there, instant message for Google is right there, so I use that all the time to work with people," says an assistant professor of media literacy. Echoing that sentiment, an assistant professor of history explained that although he has started using text messaging on all of his devices (cell phone, iPad, and so on), compared to e-mail, text messaging integrates poorly into the rest of his workflow.

The second most popular type of digital communication tool cited by respondents is Skype voice-over-IP service and instant messaging client. "I have made quite a bit of use of Skype for keeping in contact with collaborators," says a professor of astrophysics, while an assistant professor of mathematics specifics: "My Skype contact list has five family members and 25 collaborators, we generally use Skype a lot." The respondents also mentioned using Google Hangout, Facetime, iChat, and Adobe Connect, but to the lesser extent than Skype.

Archiving

Although scholars consulted in this study said they preferred e-mail communication because it creates a communicative trail, they put less effort into archiving e-mail than other materials. Only half of the interviewees across disciplines cited intentionally preserving their e-mail correspondence, while the majority of them reported actively archiving[7] and backing up other research materials important to them. The most often-used archiving solutions are hard drives and cloud-based services. These methods are frequently used in combination. An assistant professor of chemistry explained, for instance, that he uses Dropbox for archiving his daily research materials, and an external hard drive to store materials he does not need to access immediately or routinely:

> This [writings, notes] is automatically archived into Dropbox. Then all the data, correspondence, papers, and grants that I write, not the papers I've collected to read, goes through a program called *SugarSync*. It just creates automatic version backups to a cloud service that's accessible from anywhere. Papers [downloaded articles] happens to be a huge file, and that I back up to an external hard drive using *TimeMachine* on the Mac because I rarely need immediate access to that in any given time.

Although scholars across disciplines identify digital archiving as one of the most important segments of their research workflow, actual preservation practices vary along disciplinary lines. One example is that scholars in the humanities and social sciences frequently store Word documents, while their colleagues in the sciences store data files and presentation files. Yet in both of these academic groups, the most commonly archived materials are PDF files.

This finding might be linked to scholars' expectations concerning their longest-lasting scholarly contribution. Regardless of a disciplinary background, the majority of interviewees envisioned publications—books and peer-reviewed articles—as their enduring legacy. In the book-based disciplines such as humanities this approach is hardly surprising: "Philosophy is a book discipline, and books and peer-reviewed articles are still most canonical about my work. So, I see my books as my longest lasting [scholarly contribution]," said one professor of philosophy. His colleagues in the sciences and social sciences shared a similar approach. For example, an assistant professor of media studies related that she would like "a suite of books to be [her] professional and personal legacy," while an assistant professor of engineering explained that although she works in an applied field of developing online tools and apps "[her] most lasting contribution, of course, is always going to be papers."

This widespread focus on publications as legacy has several roots. One is a centuries-long history of academic publishing and its status as an official form of scholarly communication. As one of my interviewees, an assistant professor of French, put it: "I would see my lasting scholarly output as what is validated and recognized by the academy, that is, articles, chapters in books, or a book." Closely related to that is the formal academic reward system, which revolves around academic publishing as one of its pivotal points. A professor of physics explained that it the following way: "I think [about my legacy] largely in terms of the papers that I write. And that is probably a lack of imagination on my part, but it's the currency of the field." Finally, uncertainty about the permanence of digital materials gives traditional publications a status of more desirable legacy: "Books, for all of their problems of storage and all of this, last at least a thousand years. I don't think that there's anything digital that would be as long lasting," related an associate professor of comparative literature.

The emphasis on publications as legacy has several consequences for scholars' digital archiving practices. One is the previously mentioned focus on archiving PDF materials, that is, journal articles and electronic versions of books. In contrast, data archiving gets less attention, particularly in the humanities and social sciences. A professor of sociology maintained, for instance, that her journal publications would stay as the legacy, while her data would be destroyed: "I can destroy the data after five years, which is nice once it's published, and I do. So, after I retire, all my data can be destroyed. But if you think about it, these are rich datasets. It's a shame to destroy them. But what else do you do?" This question points further to some of the biggest archiving problems across disciplines, such as cost and storage capacity. A professor of biology observed that when he needs to make a copy of a large amount of data, the infrastructure that would allow him to do that is not available at his home institution, so he has to buy the storage space and manage it himself.

Another consequence of focusing on publications as materials worth of preserving is a reduced awareness of scholars' personal archiving responsibilities. Academic publications are typically archived in multiple institutional repositories, from those of the academic publishers to various university libraries, so scholars feel that preservation nonchalance on their side would not come with serious costs. "That legacy is preserved in the publisher archives and ADS [Astrophysics Data System], Thompson Reuters and things like that," said a professor of astrophysics, and a professor of anthropology similarly observed that here articles are archived in the library, while Google had digitized her books. When it comes to the question as to whose responsibility should be to ensure long-term access to their legacy, my interviewees had different views. A number of respondents maintained that it should be the publishers:" Once it's published, it [a responsible party] would be the organization that publishes it," argued a professor of comparative literature. Other respondents held, however, that such a responsibly cannot be granted to publishers, since commercial organizations do not necessarily work in the public interest: "I don't like the idea of commercial journals being responsible for that maintenance," said a professor of applied mathematics and biology, "because the commercial interests oftentimes have not fallen into alignment with the public interest." Most of my interviews believe that preservation should be the task of scholarly institutions, but they assign that task to different institutions. While scholars in the sciences believe that professional organizations should have that role, their colleagues in the humanities and social sciences focus on home institutions. "I don't have the capacity [to preserve materials], particularly nowadays in the digital age; I think the university should assume a responsibility. I'll be gone pretty soon, but the university has a right and an obligation to its memory," asserted a professor of Spanish. On the other hand, an associate professor of physics argued, for instance, that a professional organization such as the American Physical Society, would be the best solution for ensuring long-term access, because it is the organization "whose interests, and the interest of its members, would be tied up in that archive." A small number of interviewees held that preservation of their scholarship should be their personal responsibility, and those were mainly scholars in the sciences. A professor of chemistry argued, for instance, that scholars should personally assume that task, but that universities should be responsible to provide tools for easy archiving.

The issue of long-term access is also connected to scholars' visions of their academic legacy. Although most of them focused on publications, other forms of legacy were also envisioned. A professor of genetics explained, for instance, that his genetic datasets are his most valuable heritage, which has been archived in GenBank[8] through thousands of entries, ever since he deposited the first genetic sequence there in 1985. Similarly, an associate professor of computer science maintained that computer programs he is developing are his key legacy, so making those programs freely available for wide use would be the best way to ensure long-term access to that legacy. An associate professor of mathematics similarly observed that he would like his lasting scholarly output to be a meta-legacy of building connections between fields, so the best way of preserving that would be to "convince a bunch of other mathematicians that certain tools in one area of mathematics are good tools to apply to other problems." Finally, a professor of youth development expressed her views on legacy and archiving in the following way:

> The most important thing for me is to improve the lives of the kids I'm working with in Africa. You can write a billion papers and ten people will read them. But if you can actually change lives, then that, to me, is my lasting scholarly output. My real passion is just making peoples' lives better. You can't archive that anywhere.

Yet, among scholars in the humanities and social sciences archival negligence can be such that some of them do not archive and back up their research materials at all, commonly citing the lack of skill, habit, or both: "It's insane. I know it is [dangerous]. I don't have any external storage devices because I don't know how to use them, and I'm just absolutely ignorant about those [cloud-based services]," said an assistant professor of French and linguistics, adding that she often prints out electronic texts and archives hardcopies. Yet, such complete absence of preservation activities is rare. Much more frequently, scholars' archiving practices are hampered through a set of challenges, most of which correspond to those identified in Marshall's (2007) study. One of such big challenges for scholars in the humanities and social sciences is file migration and obsolete technological formats:

> I've got tape backup stuff from 1990s, but I have no machine to read it. I've got five and a quarter inch floppy drives, I've got three and a half inch floppies. This stuff is in my garage. I'm not deleting it, but it's getting trapped in that form. (Assistant professor of education)

Insufficient knowledge about how to migrate files onto new formats or how to consolidate files from different devices results in considerable data losses. As in the above quotation, a significant number of my interviewees reported having inaccessible files, most commonly as a result of not migrating to new data formats. This suggests a need for promoting personal archiving literacy among scholars (see Zastrow, 2014), as well as for developing self-archiving strategies integrated into scholars' research workflows. These strategies could include institutional repositories or institutional subscriptions to cloud storage services; the high rate of users in this study who routinely lose information due to outmoded storage formats mandates locally based institutional action to help save information for the benefit of researchers and institutions.

Another obstacle to archiving is related to privacy issues, similar to those in scholars' storage practices. "Most of my data is archived in my basement," said an associate professor of education, explaining that her research materials comprise videos of children who are identified with emotional behavior disorders, so any possibility of the videos getting outside the research group has to be prevented. For some other scholars in the humanities and social sciences, digital archiving is predicated upon the need to digitize their research materials. For instance, an associate professor of political science explained that a rich research corpus that she collected over decades includes valuable data, such as government documents and interview records, none of which had been digitized: "In terms of archiving, it would be nice if it were possible to inexpensively and quickly scan so that there would be a digital copy of those materials."

Finally, a number of scholars indicated that sharing information on the Web is their way of archiving materials. A professor of mathematics explained, for instance, that the best way to hedge against loss of data is to make sure that things are done in an open setting, so he posts his work in open-source online forums to get it distributed as widely as possible, because "when something valuable is put out there, it gets archived all over the world and then it can be reconstructed if it gets lost from one particular place." Similarly, a professor of philosophy describes his blog as a place for archiving, specifying that every time he does or publishes something, he writes a blog post about it, so "that's really a good archive."

This practice also raises the topic of sharing research data and materials, which is the next and final section in this chapter.

Sharing

Preservation of research traces is also achieved through sharing data and other research materials. A common narrative about contemporary digital scholarship juxtaposes scholars in the sciences as "sharing oriented" versus humanists and social scientists as "territorial." Yet, the findings of this study suggest that the origins of those differences are more convoluted than the stereotypes imply. For instance, this study found that academic status and specificities of objects of inquiry influence scholars' sharing practices more significantly than do their disciplinary backgrounds.

In the sciences, a majority of respondents classified data sharing as indispensable. "Certainly [I share data], I'm religious about posting things," says an associate professor of mathematics. A professor of biology underscored this view:

> [I share data] all the time. Part of my background has come from being a fruit fly biologist, and the culture there was always about sharing, not only digital stuff, but also molecular reagents and all of that sort of thing.

Scholars in the sciences commonly share data, code, research articles, as well as preprints of their publications. Those research materials are shared via e-mail, posted on scholars' personal or research teams' websites, or disseminated through code management platforms such as *GitHub* or *Bitbucket*. Preprints are shared at the time, or ahead, of submitting a paper to a journal in furtherance of disseminating the information more quickly. The respondents offered that they sometimes disseminate their data even before fully grasping it themselves simply to share their excitement and facilitate interpretation of new findings:

> If it's a result that we're excited to share, we might send raw data to communicate and say: "Oh, this is an interesting result, although we don't quite know what it is." (Professor of chemistry)

Yet, scholars in the sciences can also be territorial about their data. Among my interviewees, I recorded this tendency most often among tenure-track scholars. This finding relates directly to the academic reward system, which incentivizes publishing, not data sharing. As Fraser and Puwar (2008) stated, in contemporary academia data are an asset "which can be translated into (exchanged for) published articles, royalties, esteem-ratings, reputation, status, departmental income, promotion and invitations in the global circuits of academic productivity" (14). For tenure-track scholars, eager to produce a constant stream of publications that will populate their tenure files, research data thus become a commodity that they are not willing to share:

> Unless there is some obvious reason to share the data, I don't see any benefit in doing so, and maybe even a deficit because I don't want someone to reanalyze it and then publish it. I want them to know as much as I want to tell them about the dataset. I don't want them to know enough that they could make something better or different. The benefit of me sharing versus not sharing is right now heavily cited on not sharing. (Assistant professor of engineering)

Tenure-track scholars across disciplines are faced with heavy requirements and competition, and territoriality sometimes morphs into a survival strategy. Without an academic incentive or a funding requirement, they are hesitant to share their data. This applies even to depositing data into institutional repositories,

which are seen as holding not only the promise of data steward-
ship but also the "risk" of data dissemination:

> I guess I'm kind of territorial, protective of my dataset, so I don't
> know that I would really be willing to have the repository as a
> place where my data or information could be shared because
> I don't have to share it at this point in time. It's not federally
> funded, so I don't need to worry about that. It's mine and I can
> keep it. (Assistant professor of kinesiology)

Senior scholars, on the other hand, recognize the dangers of the
existing academic reward system and its influence on younger
scholars:

> In the narrower sense, kind of the promotion and tenure sense, it's
> the books and articles [that matter]. The measurable stuff, the sort
> of CV stuff. But I think that we're in danger of so bureaucratiz-
> ing our evaluation processes that younger faculty are driven away
> from some of the greatest contributions they could make because
> they're not immediately measurable in merit reviews. (Professor
> of rhetoric)

Regardless of their willingness to share the data, respondents in
the sciences expressed overwhelming hesitance toward any sharing that includes social media. In a stark contrast with humanities
respondents, for whom "twittering" is synonymous with "sharing," scholars in the sciences reported a consistent avoidance of
social media in both professional and private spheres. They often
viewed social media as a wasteful activity, which lacked focus in
both content and audience:

> I find a lot of the material [on social media] a waste of time. You
> have to sift through it all, and I can be doing other, more produc-
> tive things with my time. I rely on other news and media to digest
> relevant content. (Associate professor of biology)

Scientists make exceptions, however, on a focused, case-by-case
basis. For instance, an associate professor of mathematics admit-
ted that he avoids popular social media but is actively involved
in Math Overflow (see http://mathoverflow.net/), a question-

and-answer website for professional mathematicians. "This is sort of like social media, but it's very mathematically focused," this interviewee explains. Respondents in the sciences also reported occasionally using *GitHub*, which offers social media functionality targeted to their work and filters out distractions.

Among the respondents in the humanities and social sciences, sharing is less established, for various reasons. One reason stems from the character of the humanistic objects of inquiry and research practices. As my respondent emphasized, their work is usually individual and implies deep thinking about small corpora of texts, visuals, music scripts, and similar materials that are, for the most part, already available to other scholars via public or institutional records.

Still, a number of respondents in the humanities reported actively sharing information, most commonly through social media: "Sharing, is constant, I'm a Twitterer mostly," says a professor of philosophy, one among the many humanities respondents whose first definition of "sharing" is social media. In the same fashion, an associate professor of Dutch language and literature said he shares almost all of his professional activities through his blog and social media accounts. Such scholars point out that new forms of digital media sharing can be threatening to traditional approaches to scholarship, particularly print scholarship, that values cloistered life and ownership of ideas before they get revealed:

> We don't have a strong history of collaboration. We have a strong critique of the notion of authorship, but that's a theoretical critique. When it comes down to, "OK, well how are you actually authoring your papers?" well it turns out to be quite traditional. So, that's a challenge in the humanities side, for sure. (Associate professor of comparative literature)

Among my respondents, the use of social media goes beyond collegiate interaction; it affords exchanges with the wider public. "The use of digital technologies forced me to make my thoughts more accessible to a wider public," reported a professor of philosophy. He added, however, that it is increasingly important for faculty to think about their online identity and how they are being perceived online. "I realize that I'm a white male in a position of some authority in an institution, so I can probably do some things that maybe other people might not feel as comfortable doing," he adds, pointing to an increasing number of cases in which scholars' statements made through social media platforms negatively affected their professional positions.

Finally, some of the respondents recognized the pragmatic value to social media, expressing how it helps promote one's work and earn scholarly recognition in an increasingly competitive environment:

> I also use social media so that I could kind of leverage the public nature of it to market their [colleagues'] work, in the hopes that they would then, in turn, market mine. I hate to put it in such instrumentalist terms, but that's really what I was thinking. (Associate professor of history)

In some cases, the lack of sharing originates from previously mentioned academic recognition system, which favors publishing over sharing. Some of the respondents explained that they rarely feel comfortable sharing even the data from their completed and published studies, as they feel there is a lot under their purview that they might yet want to do with the data. "I would love at some point for others to analyze [my data]. That's no problem. But we're still actively looking at some of the questions that we wanted to look at first," said an associate professor of anthropology.

In some cases, however, the lack of sharing is directly related to scholars' objects and methods of inquiry, most of all to privacy issues:

> All of the work that I do cannot touch any social place at all. It has to be password-protected. I don't share any data even on e-mail. Just if I'm talking about a project, it would be over e-mail, but any actual data sharing that I could do would have to be face to face. (Associate professor of psychology)

Similarly, the respondents engaged in ethnographic research explained that their work assumes developing rapport and trust with study participants, some of whom reveal intensely personal matters, so sharing even anonymized data would feel like violating participants' privacy and trust.

For some of the respondents, discussing or sharing information via digital tools and resources feels deeply incompatible with their subject matter. For example, a professor of history told me that her teaching and research address very troubling questions of ethics and social responsibility with respect to civilian violence, and specifies:

> Having done the seminar at the Holocaust Museum, I didn't want to ever trivialize these human experiences. I find that students are very brilliant with the social media, but they don't have the historical and political understanding. When we're looking at a testimony from a genocide survivor, I don't feel comfortable to do something like a blog or use some kind of social media. I just want to return to the nature of the research that I work on.

Scholars' individual practices of sharing and using digital tools for other scholarly activities relate significantly to their disciplinary backgrounds and objects of study, which is the topic to which we turn in chapter 3.

CHAPTER 3

Disciplinary (Re)Orientations

Conceptualizing transformations in academic fields is a complex task, as neither transformations nor academic fields can be analytically approached as homogeneous and static objects of inquiry. What can be observed as a disciplinary change in one case might already be an established disciplinary practice in another case; what might appear as a transformation prompted by digital technologies could actually be a long-existing inclination brought to light by new technical means; what could be (administratively) defined as a cohesive field of study might consist of diverse, even opposed, research practices and assumptions. Therefore, disciplinary transformations proposed in this chapter are not conceived as either exhaustive or fixed categories. Rather, they are proposed as indicators of possible scholarly (re)orientations within particular communities of practice. Based on the fieldwork data, I propose and trace four areas of scholarly (re)orientations, conceived as processes of capacity building. One area concerns research capacity, another focuses on knowledge capacity, the third considers technical capacity, while the fourth area of transformation discusses value capacity in the humanities.

Research capacity

As illustrated in chapter 2, digital technologies are permeating all phases of humanists' workflow, but with different degrees of adoption and impact. These technologies are indispensable for finding and accessing information, as well as in writing research outputs, but their use in analytical and interpretative practices is still not fully established among humanists. Thaller (2012) observes that 40 years ago the use of computers in humanists' work had the same twofold role: easing routine tasks and pursuing methodological development (pp. 9–10). Decades later, digital methods have not yet achieved wider uptake in humanists' analytical work, and this is where practices of scholars in the humanities and sciences still diverge most significantly. The reasons for that are manifold. Sometimes, the roots can be sought in a traditional tale of "two cultures" (Snow, 2001/1959), and the politics of evidence that continued in later years, promoting the debates of dualism between the empirical sciences and the humanities (see Denzin and Giardina, 2008). But reasons for this can also be sought closer to the digital humanities ground, in specific activities and epistemic commitments pursued in this field.

One element is related to massive digitization efforts that shaped digital humanities for several decades. Digitizing primary materials and preparing them for easy access and advanced analytical manipulation was a necessary and commendable endeavor of numerous projects and institutions, but the downside was that human and financial resources were often exhausted in those efforts. Instead of being a phase toward analytical goals, digitization frequently ended as a goal in itself. Thaller (2012) argues that preparation of digital material was so labor exhaustive, that many projects run out of time and energy for analysis, creating one of the biggest problems in the field. With the Web capabilities developed throughout the 1990s, the activities in digital humanities shifted toward demonstratively successful digitizing efforts, and, again, away from analysis:

> While the interest in analytical possibilities [of digital humanities] was moderate, the interest in the proven possibility of having tens of thousands of pages of archival documents instantly available in the early WWW was overwhelming. (Ibid., p. 10)

This legacy of digitization as the end, not the entry point, has had effects for many years, shaping humanists' perception and use of digital resources and tools. For instance, in explaining the general purpose of developing the Ivanhoe game, McGann (2002) pointed that

> the digital technology used by humanities scholars has focused almost exclusively on methods of sorting, accessing, and disseminating large bodies of materials. In this respect the work has not engaged the central questions and concerns of the disciplines. It is largely seen as technical and pre-critical, the occupation of librarians, and archivists, and editors. (para. 1)

Deegan and Tanner (2002) similarly concluded that ease of access and immediacy were primary features attracting scholars to digital resources. A decade after these observations, humanities scholars with whom I talked still highlight easier and broader access to sources as one of the most significant developments of technology-related transformations in their areas of study. This is illustrated in the words of a professor of rhetoric and Spanish who estimates that availability of research materials that would otherwise be difficult to access is key transformation in humanists' work. Similarly, a professor of bibliographical studies considers aggregation of geographically distributed sources the main benefit of implementing digital technologies in humanities research.

Among the funders, access to research materials is also seen as an important benefit of technology use, and availability of those materials is identified as one of the most immediate and significant impacts of digital technologies on humanities scholarship:

> I think even someone who doesn't think that technology has much of an impact on their scholarship can look at how their practices have changed in the past ten years, and the ways that they have been able to get access to various materials for their own research. [Senior program officer]

Yet, the kind of change that accentuates access to research materials is also seen as just an initial step toward broader and more significant methodological and epistemological transformations in humanities scholarship. A codirector of an institute for technology in the humanities explains that a more signifi-cant scholarly change stems from analytical features that enable research materials to be not only accessible, but also analyzable, that is, intellectually accessible in ways that would be difficult to achieve otherwise.

An assistant professor of comparative literature makes a similar argument. In his area of study, easy access to digitized materials has resulted in significantly bigger datasets, but not necessarily in epistemological transformations. "My datasets are far bigger, so some people say that means the claims that we're making now are more real, more realistic," this respondent explains, and adds: "I'm very skeptical of these claims. The ways in which it [research] does change, are speed, efficiency of interactions, but the kind of interaction that's happening is the same."

Indeed, the relationship between doing traditional research faster and on a bigger scale versus developing new modes of research is an important question in digital humanities, even among the developers of well-known resources. For instance, one of the developers of the Old Bailey Online says that his "greatest frustration is that we can now answer all the questions we had in 1980 faster, much, much faster. . . . But, what we haven't yet done is develop the new questions and the new paradigms that should be possible" (cited in Bulger et al., 2011: 28).

The tension between "faster" versus "innovative" can also be seen as a question of gradual change, or—as some of my respon-dents put it, paraphrasing Keats—the question of slow time for digital humanities. This argument posits that scholars initially ask questions that they could ask without the technology, because they are not used to digital research tools and methods yet. Gradually, it leads toward new questions, which could not have been asked without the technology:

> Maybe you make a map of something that you're interested in, and then through seeing the map, you say, "oh, there's this pattern here." I never would have thought of that pattern, and now I can think of interesting new questions that I can ask about that pat-tern that I wouldn't have seen without that technology. (Associate professor of archeology)

This question concerns scholars' relation with the empirical, that is, with the recognized ways of construing and analyzing objects of inquiry. As discussed in chapter 2, the perception of digital tools and methods as "data crunching," incompatible with humanistic interpretative work, contributes to lower uptake of these technologies among humanists. Respondents in my study often describe humanists' objects of inquiry as contextualized representations incongruous with computable and retrievable data, and analytical work as "cognitive" and "deep-thinking," with writing and iterative reflexivity as main analytical processes. In this perspective, digital research tools are seen as "buckets that we can put our thoughts into" and as "data crunching machines," as some of my respondents put it. An associate professor of history explains, for instance, that cognitive tasks constitute the main part of his analytical work, while in certain projects, such as exploring differences between populations, he draws on bigger datasets: "There, you're not going to want to do that work in your head. You're going to want to have a data crunching tool to do that kind of work," he stresses. Along those lines, Porsdam (2013) recognizes a bias in digital humanities that favors *how* over *what* of knowing, and argues for the recognition of deep thinking and other traditional humanities analytical processes, that is, for establishing a balance between quantitative and qualitative methods.

Yet, it would be a mistake to assume that this is a dichotomous position. The juxtaposition of *how* versus *what* of knowing is artificial and ineffective insomuch that the *how* necessarily determines the *what* (see Law, 2004). Through fostering the scale and pace of research, digital technologies also facilitate other transformations in humanities scholarship. Among my respondents, for instance, an associate professor of Dutch literature explains that the Google Ngram Viewer phrase-usage tool[1] draws on a method that philologists have used long before digital technology, but they did it painstakingly, keeping a database on their own: "So, it [Ngram] didn't change the ability to do it; it changed the ability to do it quicker, faster," this scholar points out. However, he also emphasizes that transformation of this traditional philologists' approach into a digital method

generates important transformations in the structure of disciplinary research practice and epistemic authority:

> In the past, if you were the guy who identified the discourse
> around a particular word or keyword in the 19th Century and did
> it really well, you were this magnificent scholar who spent twenty
> years in *Bibliotheque Nationale* in France, or something like that.
> But nowadays, you type it into Ngram and you see OK, in these
> 10 years, this word was buzzing. So, we can all do that.

A number of participants in this study comparably argued that
digital humanists are first and foremost humanities scholars, and
that the designator "digital" reflects a collection of methods,
including traditional humanities methods, enhanced through
digital means. A president of one of the digital humanities associations explains that the large electronic corpora built in recent years
prompts questions that are crosscutting through a vast amount of
content and are best asked by mining electronic resources, and
acknowledges that this is the direction in which most of the digital humanities research has been developing. Yet, the respondent
underlines that it is neither only nor the most important direction
in digital humanities:

> If you asked me what a digital scholar is, I would say a scholar who
> uses digital methods in order to ask questions or explore issues
> that would be difficult to explore in other ways. That could be a
> matter of scale—to be able to mine through lots of content more
> quickly, efficiently and in a more revealing way—or it could be to
> use digital tools in an explicitly interpretive way.

This reaffirms the view of authors such as Drucker (2009), who
recognize digital humanities as "the study of ways of thinking
differently about how we know what we know and how the interpretative task of the humanist is redefined in these changed con-
ditions" (p. xii). Some of the scholars in this study posit that,
in doing digital humanities research, a starting point cannot be
the same as in traditional humanities. For instance, a professor
of information studies argues that developing a digital research
project is "a very different situation than traditional humanities

work." He argues that the precondition for harvesting benefits of digital methods in humanities research is to understand the nature of structured data and markup as a way to make explicit the interpretative actions, as well as to be in constant dialogue with a community of people who bring different expertise to digital humanities projects, often multidisciplinary in nature.

The question about epistemological potentials of digital research tools and methods sometimes taps into the debate about digital humanities as primarily text oriented, which I explored in more detail in chapter 1. In this perspective, digital research tools are seen as text-focused, that is, adapted to the needs of linguistic research communities, but not necessarily other disciplines. Providing large structured content that humanists can use across disciplines is inadequate without accompanying tools, attuned to specific disciplinary needs. One of my respondents, the chair of an international association of digital humanities, explains it in the following way:

> I do see [projects] like Franco Moretti and distant reading and data mining, and what you can do with a million books. Well, the linguistic and language communities operate through data mining methods. Most of the others don't. They are about forms of interpretation that are very iterative, and I haven't seen much by way of technology that somehow makes that better. I'm afraid that, when you leave the linguistics community, there aren't that many things.

The same question about the development of digital research tools and resources in a way that stems from research questions and interpretation has been a major theme in a team developing a digital philology project whose work I observed over several months. In the course of the meetings and project work, the discussions and activities were framed by thinking through how the various sources to be digitized would be used in research, and which kinds of questions would be posed of the sources. The goal was not simply to "digitize," in the usual sense of the term, but to build a digital resource in which data and interpretation would be linked closely together, with research practices shaping the database architecture.

Yet, a precondition for benefitting from digital research tools and methods in humanities scholarship is mastering those resources in a learned manner. I review this subject in the next section as a discussion of knowledge capacity in digital humanities.

Knowledge Capacity

When I ask my interviewees, across disciplines, where do scholars in their field of study learn to use digital research methods and tools, the undivided response is: "On their own." Some of the respondents in the sciences had computer programing instruction as part of their graduate curriculum, but once they reached the point of becoming academic researchers and/or educators, they were left to individually care for further development of their technical skills. "Learn it on our own, it's not being taught anywhere, so it's more or less what we read," explains an associate professor of chemistry. "You pick it up on the street pretty much; you might hear about it, you might read about it," confirms a professor of physics.

In the humanities, the situation is different insomuch that the majority of scholars with whom I talked have not had formal technology-related instruction at any educational level. Siemens (2013) reports a similar finding in Canada, with less than one-third of respondents attending any kind of skill-development program in digital scholarship. Like their colleagues in the sciences, humanists learn about digital research methods and tools on their own, combining different strategies, but predominantly relaying on informal channels, such as word of mouth:

> I do everything on my own, I ask around. It feels serendipitous, it's just like word of mouth, I sort of bump into it, or I hear a friend talk about it, or a colleague will shoot me an e-mail. It's not organized or strategic at all. (Associate professor of linguistics)

One after another, humanists describe the same informal learning path. Learning is linked to immediate scholars' needs, arising from specific research problems, which generally makes this way of learning preferred over organized efforts, such as library workshops, where learning is decontextualized from scholarly practice. This method also successfully makes use of one of the scholars' most scarce recourses—their time. It enables them to direct learning efforts toward tools, methods, and subjects of particular interest to them. A drawback of this approach, however, is that learning depends on a scholar's social network and its knowledge capacity. Furthermore, as a result of such targeted learning, skills can stay underdeveloped in some key aspects; for instance, a scholar might learn to code, but not how to test the code. Finally, in-group learning might generate an enclosed and insular epistemological system, which lacks diversity of information and perspectives, and at the same time depends on colleagues' readiness to share information. According to my interviewees, however, such readiness is widely present, and this learning method operates successfully in exchanging both information and experiences related to digital research tools and methods:

> You'll be talking with a colleague and they'll have some complaint about why they can't just do X. And then if you have a solution, then you share it. I think that's by and large how people become aware of these tools and what the work-arounds are for the limitations people are frustrated by. (Associate professor of Japanese)

Such examples of informal knowledge exchange do not commonly find their way into studies of humanists' collaborative or sharing practices, so a simplified image of humanists as solitary and territorial remains influential. Still, the ethos of knowledge exchange is well recognized in digital humanities, rich in community-based resources such as *Digital Humanities Questions and Answers* section of the ACH,[2] *Bamboo Digital Research Tools*,[3] and *Digital Research Tools Wiki*.[4] One of my interviewees, a founder of one of these community-based services, explains that the goal was to create a bottom-up place where scholars could ask questions and get answers. The resource was not envisioned as focused on access to primary materials, but on the social side of information sharing:

> Digital humanities has a reputation for being filled with people who are helpful and friendly, and—because there is so little formal training—we all remember what it was like to teach ourselves something from scratch.

Informal learning among humanities scholars also often takes place through engagement with students. My respondents explain that teaching prompts them to expand knowledge of digital tools and methods, and students challenge them to be up-to-date with technology. They expect professors at least to be able to digitally moderate class materials, assignments, and communication, and, in more general sense, to modernize their scholarly habits:

> I don't use Zotero, my students do. I don't know why I don't, except I'm too lazy, a lot of it's just habit. So, I'm not up to my undergrads. (Professor of library and information science)

Even those scholars who describe themselves as "technological dinosaurs" identify the need to take up digital technologies in the classroom. By way of example, a professor of French says that next time he teaches an undergraduate course he will ask someone to show him how to use the computer in the classroom, so that he could meet at least some of the expectations of his technological-savvy students. This again corresponds with Siemen's (ibid.) findings about the importance of classroom technology in humanists' work.

Humanities scholars also develop technical skills through dialogs with the classroom, or in a sort of reversed learning situation in which they learn from students. Without hesitation, my respondents explain how students teach them new digital tools and methods, helping them to broaden the scope of technical knowledge. In addition to class interaction, more formal initiatives where students teach faculty take place in digital humanities centers; I return to a more detailed discussion of this topic in chapter 4 (see pp. 119–120).

Humanities scholars who did have formal programing education were rare in this study, and they were usually found among staff at digital humanities centers, as well as among graduate students. For instance, an art historian working as the Web and database developer at a digital humanities center explains that he has been programming almost half of his life, and that having both humanities background and technical expertise enabled him to conceptualize technical answers to humanities problems, and to compose digital humanities projects. The necessity of such broader expertise is recognized and articulated in the increasing number of degree-granting programs in digital humanities, where students learn standard computer programming, database design, XML markup techniques, and so on. Among the students in traditional humanities graduate programs, the paths toward achieving such expertise were less straightforward, if at all existent. A PhD candidate in history describes her educational path in the following way:

> I have a background in programming, particularly in database design. I took a few classes in computer science, in part, I think, because my parents were a little concerned that I wanted to be a professional historian, and wanted to make sure that I came out of college with some marketable skills, if history didn't pan out. I really enjoyed programming, but went the history route.

It should also be noticed that humanists, especially in more senior generations, sometimes lose formally acquired technical knowledge, faced with the lack of possibilities to implement it. A professor of medieval studies explains, for instance, that although she had learned to code in the 1980s, she never hung on to that, as in her field of study it was not perceived as part of an academic job.

The lack of training among humanists harkens back to the question of digital technology (non)use in analytical practices. While humanists' uptake, or lack thereof, of digital tools and methods reflects certain epistemological stances, it can also be related to more mundane reasons, such as not knowing how to use a certain tool or method, and where to acquire that knowledge. This is one of the aspects where the danger, discussed in chapter 1, of dismissing "humanists with only a website" as those not belonging to digital humanities community comes to the forefront. As long as such exclusionary discourse persists, wider and epistemologically more consequential use of digital tools and methods in humanities scholarship will remain limited. Humanists are often aware of methodological and epistemological benefits of new technologies, but they are less often in a position to acquire skills and knowledge that would enable them to reach beyond search and access level and engage in more substantial research transformations. One of the interviewees puts in the following way:

> I haven't used technology in my research in a pervasive way to really, really think about epistemological issues. I'm not opposed to using technology to analyze, but I haven't had a chance to learn it. (Assistant professor of art history)

As one of the main impediments to learning digital research skills, humanists commonly identify the lack of time. One aspect of this is the learning curve, and a perception that the time needed to learn new tools and methods slows down their established research process:

> I find that I'm moving forward [in my research], and learning those protocols would cause me to pause, and I don't have time. It's like I already know what I'm doing, so I'll just do it the way I know. I felt like it [digital technology] wasn't saving me any time, and it wasn't really helping me to find new things. [Assistant professor of media studies]

This confirms Madsen's (2010) observation that humanists adopt digital tools and methods when they accelerate or simplify their research tasks, that is, when the benefit of using technology obviously surpasses nonuse. Indeed, the assumption that use of digital tools and methods would mean one more task in their already too busy work schedules is often a source of resistance among humanists toward digital scholarship. University programs aimed at promoting digital research take those considerations seriously. As one respondent puts it, the initial step at promoting a digital humanities center at his university was to assure humanists that the center was not trying to "come up with a way for people to produce more work and less time, because that's a common understanding of technology."

Another cause of researchers' lack of time for developing computational skills stems from the structure of disciplinary incentives and rewards in humanities disciplines. By way of example, an assistant professor of linguistics underscores that when a training session on digital research tools and methods is organized at his university, hardly any of the tenure-track faculty attend it, as they generally consider it a waste of time. He explains:

> We're not rewarded for doing that. What we're rewarded for is publishing, and going to one of those sessions takes away [time] from our publishing. So, there's a lot of resistance.

With digital skills still having an unrecognized status in their disciplines and departments, my interviewees say that the only organized educational initiatives at their disposal are training sessions at university libraries. Indeed, a director of digital research and scholarship at one university library explains that part of their mission, funded by university administration, is to offer formal training to humanities scholars, including "dirty software workshops," that is, programming. Humanists in my study had a mixed reaction to this approach. While some said the library sessions were "eye-opening," others did not find them so helpful. An associate professor of French says, for instance, that in his experience the librarians mostly focus on digital resources, and when it comes to research questions, it goes out of their scope, and falls into the field-specialist area. My respondents overwhelmingly consider working with colleagues as a more effective way to develop digital skills than attending library workshops or instruction sessions. An assistant professor of English explains it in the following way:

> It's such an individualized thing, what a particular person needs and where they're at in their learning process, and those classes are so generic that it just misses the mark a lot. So, learning about new tools and methods would be from colleagues mostly.

Among my respondents, the preferred type of instruction is the one that does not profess to teaching about digital technologies, but about a specific humanities subject area, introducing digital tools and methods along the way. "It's much more organic learning," one of the scholars summarizes. Attending library and similar workshops is thus seen as less effective than attending academic conferences where peers present results achieved through digital methods and tools. Learning by example inspires humanists to discover new tools and methods, and to apply them in their own work.

The orientation on learning from colleagues is probably best summarized in the words of this respondent:

> In an ideal world, I would like to see humanists teaching other humanists how to conduct research using the enhancements of digital tools; I guess that's as opposed to we bring the IT people in to teach us. I think that it should happen the way that we teach other things in the humanities, through collaboration with one another. (Professor of Romance languages and literature)

One difficulty of this approach is scholars' previously mentioned lack of time. For typically overburdened scholars, taking on an

Figure 3.1 Humanists learning from each other.

extracurricular teaching assignment of instructing peers is often outside of their capacity. Another obstacle goes in the opposite direction, stemming from colleagues' reluctance to be on the receiving end of such knowledge exchange. A professor of English and a director of an institute for technology in the humanities recalls that he used to go to every departmental meeting giving "inspirational speeches" to his colleagues about what could be done with digital research tools and methods, and encouraging them to get involved. "But I've sort of given up on evangelizing," he stresses and adds:

> If people are successful as academics already, they've been successful doing what they do. If they're successful academics, they also are busier than anybody from the outside could ever imagine. So, why would these people, since they're successful already, want to do something in a different way when they can do what they've been doing, and where are they going to get the time to do it?

Indeed, inspiring and justifying change of already established research practices is a recurrent source of struggle in digital scholarship. This problem can be framed as the question of value capacity, discussed in the following section.

Value Capacity

Disciplinary values and assumptions that scholars subscribe to significantly influence their uptake of new tools and methods (see Forsythe, 2001). Effects of scholarly values on technology adoption decisions have also been examined in digital humanities (see Collins et al., 2012). This discussion has often been framed around innovative nature of digital humanities, and the need for traditionally structured disciplines to adapt to a novel, and presumably advanced, scholarly environment. As Gold (2012) puts it,

> At stake in the rise of the digital humanities is not only the viability of new research methods (such as algorithmic approaches to large humanities data sets) or new pedagogical activities ... but also key elements of the larger academic ecosystem that supports

such work. Whether one looks at the status of peer review, the evolving nature of authorship and collaboration, the fundamental interpretative methodologies of humanities disciplines, or the controversies over tenure and casualized academic labor that have increasingly rent the fabric of university life, it is easy to see that the academy is shifting in significant ways. (ix)

Indeed, authorized disciplinary ways of knowing and working significantly affect scholars' practices in this new academic ecosystem, both through informal peer attitudes, and through formal system of certification. A professor of philosophy says, for instance, that in his discipline a scholar doing digital research runs a risk of not being taken seriously, because of a common preconception that digital research lacks rigor of traditional scholarship:

> I worry about that, and part of my strategy as a now full professor and a tenured person and even as an associate dean, is to model digital scholarship that's rigorous, and to try to illustrate an example of how it might be done.

Pointing out that philosophy is traditionally a book discipline, and peer-reviewed manuscripts are most canonical, he stresses that he works hard to craft scholarly outputs that meet those criteria. But a significant part of his work is also devoted to developing a website and a podcast of digital dialogs, which cultivate the traditional philosophical dialog in the digital age. Yet, because digital dialogs are not peer-reviewed in the traditional sense, they only indirectly become part of his academic recognition: "The way I get credit for them academically now is how they enrich my traditional scholarship," this respondent underscores, and adds:

> I have intentionally pursued the kind of dual tracks of continuing to publish in traditional ways, always trying to enrich that with the digital component, and then try to find models of digital communication, digital publication, digital scholarly communication that would be paradigm to a rigorous academic scholarship.

This statement resonates with a growing debate about digital humanists needing to double their efforts as to get relevant academic recognition (see Dunn, 2014). My respondents emphasize that this is an acute problem. Junior faculty interested in doing digital humanities work are evaluated by senior colleagues, who vote on their tenure-committees, and who are not easily convinced that work that takes digital form is serious scholarship. Thus, most of the junior scholars get advised to write a book, as a recognized and tenurable research output, and to wait until they get tenured if they want to pursue digital scholarship. "So, we're in a kind of vicious cycle," says a professor of English and the chair of a digital humanities association, and adds:

> It inhibits the younger people, who have to be twice as productive. They do their digital stuff, but they also keep on going with their book, because the book is the guarantee, and the other stuff is really iffy. And this gets into another loop, which is that right now, the only way the old guard can be convinced that new digital work is valuable scholarship is through peer reviewing as they know it. So, here we are, a field that's trying to transform the whole notion of peer review, stuck in a place where, unless they use the old form of peer review, the young people can't get credit.

In addition to traditional disciplinary systems of accreditation and quality control, established ways of working undergo transformations, too. In the humanities, one of the most important changes concerns the transition from solitary to collaborative work. A number of my humanities respondents perceive solitary work as a defining feature of humanities epistemology and methodology. "The model in the social sciences is much more to do collaborative research, and, of course, it's the model in Engineering," posits an assistant professor of French and linguistics, and adds:

> But the humanities model, until fairly recently, had a whole hierarchy of value associated with joint works versus individually authored. And I think that there are cultural values within a given discipline, and the humanities' dominant value still is that it's an individually authored thing.

As a point of comparison, respondents in the sciences overwhelmingly highlighted increased collaboration as one of the most important and most beneficial effects of digital technologies on their work. For instance, an assistant professor of mathematics stresses that 80 percent of the papers he has written are collaborative, and that in Mathematics the amount of collaboration is massively increasing:

> Twenty years ago, the majority of mathematics papers were solo papers. We crossed this boundary where the majority of papers are not solo papers anymore a couple years ago. I think this digital technology, especially in the last ten years, has been really increasing collaboration.

Contrary to this, the majority of interviewees in the humanities said that, despite such increased possibilities for collaboration brought by digital tools, they still work individually:

> I certainly see a lot of talk in the Chronicle [of Higher Education] about how the humanities are going to be more collaborative, and for some people they probably are. But the sort of work I have done is pretty traditional. It's my sweating it out and figuring out what I want to say and saying it, and it's what I've done and been trained to do. [Professor of French and gender studies]

Such persistence of traditional scholarly assumptions and practices is sometimes seen as conservative and detrimental for humanities current and future efforts. Voices calling for "revolutionary change" in the humanities are thus not uncommon. For instance, while Parry (2010) proclaims that he does not want "a digital facelift for the humanities," but wants "the digital to completely change what it means to be a humanities scholar," Bogost (2010) adds that it is not the humanities, but the humanists who need to change, and proposes a method:

> We must be brutal. We must invoke wrath instead of liberation. We must cull. We must burn away the dead wood to let new growth flourish. If we don't, we will suffocate under the noxious rot of our own decay. (para. 10)

Similar revolutionary voices can also be heard among my interviewees. One of them puts it in a blatant way: "These situations will be handled one funeral at the time." Another takes a more congenial approach:

> Eventually, the older scholars would retire and then over the course of a generation, younger, more technologically savvy students would become the new crop of professors. And, therefore, there would be a major change in the humanities disciplines.

Yet, challenges arising from a tendency to automatically dismiss digital scholarship can also be turned around, toward trends of embracing it in an equally uncritical manner. As long as a dilemma of weather to be or not to be digital is seen as normative, with its double-edged sword cutting at both alleged technophiles and technophobes, it will be difficult to synthesize traditional and emerging forms of humanities knowledge production into a cohesive field. For instance, the resistance among some of the humanists toward digital scholarship does not have to be seen as an obstacle to the development of digital humanities. Instead, it can be brought into play as an opportunity. "When you understand it [resistance] in its disciplinary context, it doesn't seem as backwards," says a professor of Romance languages and literature. Humanities scholars, who are trained to do critique, to be skeptical, and to question things instead to accept them point-blank, can provide a constructive challenge of digital scholarship.

Furthermore, in order to create knowledge capacity in the humanities that includes the digital component, it is important to have enough successful models of digital research that are answering important humanities questions, and in a compelling way. A professor of English and the chair of a digital humanities association puts it in the following way:

> This is the key question [in digital humanities], and I think the number-one concern that emerged in a lot of different places—where is our proof that we're doing valuable work? How can you document it? And there aren't really many good answers.

In his view, the field of digital humanities has two important questions to answer: (1) how can it help humanities researchers do better what they have already been doing and (2) what kinds of new things will researchers be able to do.

Overwhelmingly, my respondents highlight that the humanities disciplines need to have a set of evaluation criteria for digital scholarship, just as they do for traditional scholarship, where they would be able to assess what is the intellectual value of a piece of digital work, how is it contributing to the field, what are the research methods, and so on:

> People don't know how to evaluate digital materials, they have not historically considered them the same category as things like books or traditional print publications. We don't have good peer-review mechanisms for either digital resources or digital research work.

The lack of formally established review mechanisms and criteria is sometimes substituted with alternative accreditation mechanisms, such as funding agencies' decisions. Those agencies become stamps of approval in both internal digital humanities efforts, and in their interactions with traditional departmental and review systems:

> Since we [digital humanities] don't have robust peer-review mechanisms and things like that, if a funding agency gives you money, that's a good seal of approval, this is a good project. And you could go back to your institution and your department and say, "Look, they gave me $100,000 to do this project, they think it's good. I'm not just telling you anymore—a big agency has said it."

Such an approach, however, puts a big burden of responsibility on funding agencies, and also opens the door to an unwanted possibility of funders' decisions guiding the work in digital humanities. In point of fact, program officers who participated in this study said they are trying to keep their ears to the ground, and be aware of the tensions and discussions in digital humanities, since the field is the one that needs to help them decide what is important and worth of support:

> We still follow the endowment model with the importance of peer review, and we want our peer reviewers to guide us with their advice, which projects they feel would better serve the community as opposed to others. [Senior program officer]

The question of agreed upon evaluation criteria and mechanisms in digital humanities thus becomes a crucial issue for all parties involved—scholars, universities, academic publishers, and funders. Yet, in a field that cannot easily decide even on its own definition, it does not seem likely that establishing a set of undisputed, joint criteria and mechanisms would be in any way easier, if at all possible:

> Digital humanities increasingly need good criteria for assessing the intellectual content of the project. And we have talked about this for ten years, other people have probably talked about for longer. We need to be able to have a set of criteria that say what is the intellectual value here, what's it contributing to the field, where's the new knowledge, what are the research methods, are they sound, is it well positioned within its field? So, real basic things that are not hard to answer, but I think many people trained traditionally don't feel they have a grounding for making those assessments. We need a bridge culture to do that, so that it's not a silo within the humanities. (Director of a digtial humanities center)

An additional challenge is that, without a theoretical debate concerning relevant evaluation criteria and connected epistemological and methodological questions, the field of digital humanities runs the risk of overemphasizing the applied nature of its work. This goes back to the still unresolved debate about making, building, and theorizing in digital humanities, where different scholars and schools of thought advocate for contradictory approaches (see chapter 1). Among the respondents in this study, a common position holds that digital humanities constitutes an applied field, but that digital humanists are also people who theorize the work they are doing. "The important thing is that the digital things we create . . . have to be an object of our study," underscores the chair of an alliance of digital humanities.

The importance of synchronizing the theoretical and applied nature of digital humanities is best seen in the activities of developing digital research tools and resources for humanities scholarship, which are examined in the following and concluding section of this chapter.

Technical Capacity

When discussing digital research tools and resources, the point of departure in this study is to observe them as epistemic tools, conceived as an analytic complement to the concept of epistemic objects (see Rheinberger, 1997). While epistemic objects generate new questions, the term "tool" is used here to indicate that digital research tools also suggest the potential of new ways of answering, that is, encourage new research practices and epistemologies. In the same way as research methods create social reality they are set to investigate (see Law, 2004), digital research tools shape both the object of inquiry and the way(s) of knowing it. Therefore, digital scholarship is not merely supported by technology, but constituted through it. In the sciences, where digital research tools have longer and more prominent history of use than in the humanities, the influence of digital research tools on disciplinary research practices and epistemologies, as well as on cognitive processes, has been well documented (see Beaulieu, 2003; Hagen, 2001; Bowker, 2000).

This study focuses on two questions of tool development: (1) what features should a digital research tool have to be useful in the humanities; (2) what kind of influence do humanities scholars have on the process of digital research tool development. The results indicate that humanities scholars have minimal, if any, impact on tool development, but they do have rather well-defined views on preferred qualities of a digital research tool.

In the view of my interviewees, wide interconnectedness is one of the most desired elements that digital research tools and resources should have. Instead of using separate tools for different phases of the workflow, as it is currently the case, humanities scholars envision tools that would enable seamless and multidimensional flow of research activities from one phase to another and back, across multisided and multimedia corpora. A professor of philosophy says that he wants a tool to get his full research circle closed, where he can go from searching, through annotation and everything else to publication. Similarly, an assistant professor of English describes her preferred research tool in the following way:

> In one interface, it would have the ability to store data and help me to analyze it in a really organized way that I could go back and play around with. It would also allow me to develop a bibliography and to keep notes and articles and things, works that I'm reading, and annotate, and so forth. So, it would have both [data and tools] all together.

Academics who hold functions in digital humanities organizations, and thus have insights into a broader set of humanities research projects and discussions, make the same point, accentuating the importance of interconnected corpora and associated tools. The president of an association for the humanities and the chair of an alliance of digital humanities both underscore that key element of a successful digital resource is content that is specific to humanists' needs, and big enough to enable complex queries across that corpora. However, they point out that even the most massive digital resources in digital humanities do not have enough content for that type of complex analysis. Only when interlinked with other resource, such as special library collections and academic databases, they enable researchers to compose queries that mine the primary and secondary sources in more advanced analytic ways.

In addition to interlinked corpora, efficient digital resources should incorporate tools for the analysis of that content. "You need to have tools that are visibly available with the content," argues the chair of the alliance of digital humanities. Those tools need to be intuitive and easy to use, he adds, corroborating thus the view about the importance of simplicity in technology use universally held among the academics who participated in this study:

> If you try to use one [tool], and you start getting messages like "you've got to do this" and then "you've got to do that," and maybe it won't quite work, and it needs tweaking, you lose humanities scholars right away. [Professor of history]

In addition to easiness of use, a tool should also be easy to learn and simple to curate. As discussed earlier, the lack of time is one of the most common barriers to development of digital skills among the humanities scholars, so a shorter learning curve with a broader area of application makes for a more desired humanities research tool. As a professor of information studies points out, "It [a digital research tool] has to be very low threshold and very high ceiling, and that's pretty much a shared conception [among humanities scholars]."

Other desired features of a digital research tool include interoperability, open standard, and sustainability. These three elements are interrelated, and they facilitate realization of a seamless research workflow. While interoperability enables easy exchange of data via a common set of exchange protocols, open standard provides for interoperability by design, in which the common protocol is defined and implemented in advance. Combined, these two features provide for easier and more efficient sustainability of digital tools and resources.

In the area of digital humanities, the interplay of interoperability, openness, and sustainability is sometimes observed in a difference between "boutique" and "generic" tools. Boutique tools are commonly associated with a particular research project or a research group, and they do not intend to have wider uptake outside those boundaries. In contrast, generic tools are associated with a particular research activity or method, which makes them more universally applicable.

Among the participants in this study, boutique tools are not perceived as a desired direction in digital research tool development. "I think the most fundamental challenge [in digital humanities] is to stop doing boutique projects and start thinking about some of the benefits of designing things in common platforms," says a professor of visual studies. In the same way, the president of an association for the humanities points out that tool interoperability is critical, and it cannot be achieved through boutique projects:

> It [a digital tool] needs to be interoperable. And it needs to be sustainable, which means not so boutique that the success or failure of a particular tool depends on the three or four scholars who use it and love it.

Still, although the niche for such tools is recognized, she points out that although generic tools have better potential to meet research needs of a broader set of humanists, there is also space for a smaller-scale and more experimental tool building, which often has more vigorous capacity for innovation. The same approach is expressed in the words of the program officers at funding agencies. They stress that wider applicability and sustainability are among the key evaluation criteria they use when funding tool development, but they also support start-up tool building programs, in which the goal is not to develop a widely used and sustainable tool, but to focus on the tool development methods and processes.

Although generic tools are considered more beneficial, they are not immune to certain types of critique. For instance, an academic technology specialist argues that orientation on generic platforms can lead into a trap of trying to develop "one-size-fits-all" technical solutions, which has been a massive problem of tool development in the last couple of decades. Instead, interoperability and wider applicability should be understood in terms of flexibility and loose structure, in which users freely select, add, delete, and operate a set of research apps working in the same platform. Through that kind of tool development, "you let the community help to define what works, and that [tool] tends to get better," this interviewee concludes.

While tool features such as ease of use, interoperability, and sustainability are preferred across disciplines, openness to uncertainty is a tool attribute specifically related to humanities. The respondents posit that the main challenge of developing research tools for humanities is to balance the need for precision, which enables scholars to put together queries that deliver precise meaning, and the need for ambiguity and serendipity of humanities inquiry.

For instance, a professor of bibliography argues that ambiguity and uncertainty constitute the highest analytical level that needs to be built into humanities research tools:

> Not only do we tolerate them [ambiguity and uncertainty], but it was our interest in these kinds of approaches—to reading rather than knowledge, to experience rather than empirical evidence— that made us into humanists.

However, having such humanistic values built into digital research tools is not easy, predominantly because of the lack of humanities scholars' involvement in the tool development process.

Figure 3.2 Pursuing humanistic ambiguity across media.

Among the humanities scholars who participated in this study, the unanimous view was that experts from their disciplines have marginal, if any, influence on the development of digital research tools. In the area of commercial tools, humanists feel they might only have influence as consumers, in line with the consumer choice and demand curve dynamics. Yet, even this standard market logic does not actually give desired results, as illustrated in a case of one College of Liberal Arts I observed, and which decided to stop using a commercial digital research tool for video analysis because of the lack of interaction with the tool developer, and the developer's disregard for feedback from the college users:

> The people that have designed [the tool] designed it for work with clients who spend $15,000 for a license. And so, when they say, 'We want these modifications made,' it's done and it's out. For our college, it's not. [Associate professor of English]

Similarly, the president of an association for the humanities points to big commercial projects, such as Google Books, as prime examples that the target audience of such massive resources and financial investments was not brought into the process of thinking about the best standards for their development, and she adds that such examples could be a powerful lesson for humanities scholars.

In the area of academically developed tools, humanists have a certain kind of involvement in the development process, but it can be rather sporadic and related to beta-testing, not to earlier stages of tool building. For instance, a professor of philosophy says it is rare for scholars in his field of study to have influence on tool development, and stresses that he was grateful to be invited as a beta-tester for a university repository:

> That takes time, but I love to see what your suggestions are actually getting adopted. I think we don't have in philosophy a core cohort of people who actually are advising developers. And I think that should happen.

It is important to note that some of the scholars in the sciences have reactions similar to those of their humanities colleagues when it comes to their influence on research tool development. As an example, an associate professor of biology complains: "We seem to have no influence at all, because no one talks to us, or asks us, or listens to us." However, an important difference between the humanities and science scholars is that the latter often personally develop digital tools for their research use. "We're the ones developing them [digital research tools]," says an associate professor of chemistry, and a professor of statistics corroborates: "I write my own code, we develop our software." In that sense, researchers in the sciences have sounder influence on epistemic and methodological features built into digital research tools they use in their research practice.

Humanities scholars, on the other hand, commonly lack the skills to build their own research tools, so they either depend on software developers to build tools for them, or to collaborate in the development process. This kind of interdisciplinary collaboration is increasingly present in contemporary academia, although not without challenges. The chair of an alliance of digital humanities recalls that such collaborations were not common ten years ago, and adds,

> Even now, when we work with them, what computer science recognizes as research and what digital humanities recognizes as research are different things. So, you have to find a common set of research goals, but back then, there was not even the possibility of a dialogue.

One of the commonly mentioned reasons for the humanists' lack of involvement in the tool development is their lack of technical expertise. This is illustrated in the position of the president of an association for the humanities, who argues that humanities scholars and professional societies are not digitally savvy enough to articulate the needs of those scholars, and to effectively lobby groups such as the Library of Congress, or commercial groups like Google, about the things that humanists need. Similarly, a professor of Spanish and comparative literature posits that humanities scholars lack a frame within which to say what they might expect, or what they might want, in a way that would help development process. A professor of musicology argues that "the hard nut to crack" is to get humanists see the power of digital tools for enriching their own research, and to take a more active role in the development process.

The need for humanists' involvement in the tool development process is not merely a technical or a policy issue. It is a much broader question concerning the kind of research practices and ways of knowing these epistemic tools will promote, as well as disciplinary transformations they might prompt. In Beaulieu's (2003) words, it is the question about the configuration of technology and research practices, which reshapes expectations about both how we can know and what we can know (p. 388). In the perspective of humanities scholars, it is the question of preserving humanities epistemic values in the digital age. An academic technology specialist postulates that at the encounter of humanistic approaches and computational methods, the humanists commonly surrender to the computational "epistemic cultures of formalization" (see van Zundert et al., 2013). The danger of this a professor of art history, and a cofounder of a Digital Humanities Lab, describes in the following way:

> Unless humanists take seriously two things—the value of their own contributions to the migration of cultural legacy to the digital environment, and two, the real essential value of humanistic perspectives on the nature of knowledge—then these [digital tools] will be built without humanists, and that will be a huge mistake. If humanists are not involved, then humanistic values— which have to do with the privileging of inquiry based on ambiguity and tolerance of uncertainty and uncertain outcomes—will be pushed to the side through the acclaims to authority of scientific and social scientific methods that believe in a production of the notion of certainty. It's not why do the humanities matter, but how do humanities matter that we need to put forward.

In the landscape of contemporary scholarship, in which interdisciplinary and technologically intensive research is increasingly becoming a new normal, the question of how do humanities matter inevitably transcends both individual and disciplinary levels of practice, and transforms into a set of organizational questions. For instance, the issues of knowledge and technology capacity building in the humanities can only be addressed within broader initiatives of institutional transformations. Those transformations are discussed in chapter 4.

CHAPTER 4

Organizational Patterns

Understanding where digital humanities (DH) as a field and a set of practices best fits into the university and academic experience takes us along a meandering organizational road. The empirical search for this answer crosses paths with institutional policies and politics, funding schemes and methods of classifying expertise and labor. This chapter provides a macro level analysis of the practices and challenges of (re)organizing humanities' academic activities, research units, services, and administrative hierarchies with respect to DH and digital scholarship. Specifically, it considers a set of organizational practices related to DH centers; the analysis focuses on DH centers rather than on educational programs because my study emphasized research practices.

Digital humanities centers emerged as an academic organizational unit in the 1980s (see Zorich, 2008). Today, they vary in size and activities but "collectively they may be characterized as entities where new media and technologies are used for humanities-based research, teaching, and intellectual engagement and experimentation" (ibid: 70). Emphasizing the role of DH centers in the humanists' transition toward digital scholarship, Fraistat (2012) posits that these centers represent "key sites for bridging the daunting gap between new technology and humanities scholars" (p. 281).

Over the past three decades, a growing number of academic institutions developed DH centers. Yet, these centers still represent an emerging and peripheral initiative in the humanities rather than a widely accepted practice. As mentioned in chapter 1, Terras's (2012) global survey of DH centers identified 114 centers located in 24 countries; two-thirds of these centers were in three countries—the United States, Canada, and the United Kingdom—and only one-third in the remaining 21 countries. *CenterNet*, an international network of DH centers, lists a higher number of centers around the world, but it also includes established academic organizations, such as American Historical Association and British Academy, and thus is not specifically representative of DH centers. Posner (2013) estimates that institutional support for DH work is still expanding, with a comparatively small number of institutions offering dedicated DH centers.

Despite their relatively slow growth, DH centers have played an important role in the evolution of technologically supported humanities scholarship. They have lead the way in developing cutting-edge resources and tools, and created pathways for providing educational, technical, legal, and advocacy support. It is thus valuable to look more closely at the organizational experiences of these academic units in order to identify best practices academic institutions could follow in promoting digital scholarship.

In this chapter, I draw data and conclusions based on my ethnographic study conducted at 11 DH centers. The sites included units recognized as pioneers of the DH center movement, as well as those that were still in the making when I visited. All centers are affiliated with research-intensive universities, have a dedicated physical space, and employ between 5 and 15 staff members. Most of these staff members are traditionally trained humanists with advanced computational skills, while a small number have backgrounds in computer sciences or social sciences. A significant number of staff hold PhDs.

This chapter begins with a close look at the goals and organizational processes upon which DH centers are developed, and then turns to discussing outreach, user support, alternative academic tracks, and other elements of the work DH centers pursue. The chapter concludes by exploring the vision of DH that organizational changes articulated through DH centers imply, and the ways in which the imagining of DH might shape future institutional changes in academia.

Goals and Positioning

A common narrative across the DH centers I visited is that they associate their foundational goals with a broad task of promoting humanities scholarship in the digital age. Sometimes, these goals are as ambitious as wanting to "revolutionize the way humanities scholars are doing their work," and sometimes articulated as more modest efforts to "inspire humanists to think about digital technologies." Whatever the exact nature of their mission, DH centers are envisioned as agents of change that "take the lead in scholarly innovation and disciplinary transformation" (Fraistat, 2012: 288).

A closer ethnographic look at DH centers, however, reveals that "transformation" and "innovation" are highly context-dependent concepts with diverse meanings. This insight should not come as a surprise, given that diffusion of innovations commonly assumes contextualized patterns and dynamics of emergence (Rogers, 2003[1962]). Contextualized dynamics of emergence unfolds across DH centers based on several factors, such as the financial, technical, and social capacities of an institution, as well as the willingness of university administrators to invest in new research units. The empirical data gleaned from this study highlight the various directions in which those different development tracks unfold in both synchronic and diachronic perspectives.

Diachronically, the DH centers I analyzed were founded from the early 1990s to present date. A significant difference on the diachronic axes is the bottom-up character of the early initiatives contrasted against the top-down nature of newer centers. In the early days, small groups of scholars, not necessarily humanists, initiated DH centers. A codirector of one of such center described its emergence in the early 1990s in the following way:

> Two of the computer science faculty received a grant from IBM that was going to allow them to do something pretty much of their own design. And they were looking around to do something different than the usual kind of computer science things. So, they hit on the idea of trying to do something for the humanities, and they created the institute.

The goal of this initiative was to provide fellowships and research support to humanities faculty wanting to investigate how technology could transform their scholarship. The inherent thesis was that transforming faculty research practices would influence their students' work and, together, these two shifts would gradually encourage broader transformations in humanists' research and teaching practices.

The center began working with just a few projects, but quickly multiplied its efforts. This initiative was so successful that it inspired national and international development of several DH centers using the same operating model. At one spin-off center, the interviewees explained:

> This place was the creation of two of us, humanities faculty, who had gone to see projects [at the previously described center] just when they were starting. In those days, computer scientists at your own university wouldn't even want to talk to you. So, you looked around for some expertise, and there wasn't any. After five years, our university finally invested, and that made [the center] possible, but it was a bottom-up thing. It wasn't the university saying, "We need to have one of those things; give us a digital humanities center."

Contrary to these early initiatives, the DH centers that followed employed top-down organizational models, prompted by the positive results of early enterprises and increasing funding for digital scholarship. Top-down initiatives had several organizational components, one being the transformation of university tech-support services into digital scholarship centers:

> Our center grew out of what was formerly called a computing facility. In 2000, it was converted into a center, which was meant to focus on becoming a hub for innovation, for fostering research and digital projects. The idea was to hire a faculty director, someone with a reputation in both humanities and preferably with a digital component to it, and for that person to lead the vision of what kind of research would be undertaken. (Director of the center)

To clarify, the faculty director who was hired to lead the unit described above left that role soon after the center opened. After a few unsuccessful searches for his replacement, the university simply abandoned the idea of creating a research innovation hub. Instead, leadership decided to position the unit as a center for technology in humanities instruction.

Another common organizational strategy of top-down initiatives was merging university IT divisions and library centers into DH research units. However, this strategy was occasionally based on the perception of DH as a "shadowy subject between humanities and computing" (see Thaller, 2012), with equally vague expectations as to the benefits of the merger:

> The impetus for establishing the center was *to see what would happen* if we moved central IT and the library closer together around supporting digital humanities, and *could the sum of these centers be greater than having them separate.* (Director of a DH center; emphasis added)

One reason top-down initiatives seemed unstructured relates to the difficulties in defining the field of DH and its scope, as described in chapter 1. One interviewee illustrated this challenge by revealing how she inadvertently became a DH librarian:

> I was the librarian for literature and history, and my boss has been reorganizing and trying new things, and he said one day, "Well, why don't we just add the words 'digital humanities' to the end of your job title and see what happens?" And within two weeks or so, I had like six hours of meetings per month that I didn't have before.

Digital humanities centers are often located in close proximity to university libraries, which could stem from the library's vital role in the humanities, but could also derive from changing patterns of library use that freed up physical spaces and organizational capabilities (see Svensson, 2010). For instance, at one of my research sites, the primary library space within the building was relocated. The vacant wing was repurposed as the new DH center and administered through a partnership between the library and the university's central IT division. At other research sites I studied, the respondents also noted that competition for unused library spaces was intense. As one interviewee stated, "Only either the most prestigious or the most important, whatever that means, get to use that space, and that's a question that we're grappling with—who gets to use it and for what purposes?"

Centers for DH increasingly win this competition for prime university library spaces, albeit not always with clearly defined purposes or identified audiences. For instance, the director of one of the centers described its formative period as follows:

> My predecessor came to [the university] with the mission of getting this [center] together. He formed the center and then took another job; he left pretty much the week that the center opened its doors. So, the center opened, but didn't have a very clear sense, from a digital humanities perspective, of how best to target services to that community. When we just threw the doors open without a clear sense of who we're targeting services to, the undergraduate community saw the monitors were the biggest around and moved in. Graduate students and faculty would poke their heads in the door and see Facebooking undergraduates, and didn't really use the space like we thought that they would.

As in the previously described example where a DH center grew out of a computing facility, university administrators here also wanted to establish a hub of scholarly innovation. However, they lacked a clear sense of what that innovation entailed, what the center's fundamental function would be, the range of services it should provide, and who would comprise its primary users. Furthermore, neither of these universities engaged the wider university community in the planning process before investing into the organizational changes. Instead, they relied on select individuals to develop the core structure and operation of the new research centers. When those individuals stepped down, the newly formed centers were left with skilled IT and librarian personnel in brand new spaces, but without goals or users.

This apparent lack of careful long-term planning could be attributed to the inexperience of an emerging academic field, still dominated with ambiguities, and struggling to define best practices for organizing DH centers. In the early phases of the diffusion of innovations, organizational failures are relatively common and at least understandable post hoc (see Rogers, 2003 [1962]). But in the two cases presented here, organizational failure could also—or even rather—be explained through the administrators' alienation from practice, where the vague motivation to join a burgeoning field steered the development. As Svensson (2010) warns, somewhat sardonically, DH initiatives, especially in their early phases, may risk "focusing on strategic-level issues at the expense of the more mundane issues such as actual research and real implementation. Put differently, there may be a gap between strategy, politics and grand visions and the grounding found in individual and institutional practice." (para. 74)

To better illustrate the consequences of poor organizational planning, I offer examples of DH centers that theoretically had the advantage of learning from others' failures. This group consisted of DH centers that were either still under development or recently launched at the time of my visit. The university administrators developing them were able to study and observe other organizational strategies, including the cases described above, and to distinguish efficient approaches from futile ones. Despite the opportunity for hindsight, some of the in-progress centers I visited still lacked strategic planning and organization.

Space was often the first consideration in conceptualizing new DH centers. At one center, housed in the university library, new glass walls represented visually transparent boundary between the print and the electronic materials. Flexible workspaces with standing stations equipped with high-end technologies were designed to adjust to user needs. But while design, ergonomic, and technical features of the center were meticulously considered, the goals for the center and thoughts about the intended user community were given far less attention during the planning phase:

> That's really a big question for us, figuring out what kind of services we want to offer. We're still trying to figure out what our service model will be, what our outreach will have to be to scholars to get them to use this. I mean, we're not sure what's going to happen on the first day when we open the doors. Are people going to know what to do? Are they going to come in, sit down,

and check e-mail? I know a big improvement is just going to be that it's going to be a beautiful space compared to what we had. (Director of the center)

In contrast to this "build first, contemplate later" approach, another campus of the same university system simultaneously launched its DH center using a very different organizational strategy. The idea to establish the center came from humanities scholars, the ultimate users, rather than from the university administration. This bottom-up enterprise mirrored those of successful DH centers created in the early 1990s. This dedicated group of scholars began the planning phase with a university-wide dialogue. They included their colleagues from the humanities division, information technologists, computer scientists, librarians, digital librarians, and other potential stakeholders. These early conversations helped identify which organizational strategies and design possibilities were consistent with their goals for the center. Further, they prioritized talking to humanities students and faculty about their visions, wishes, and potential points of resistance related to the center. Their comprehensive planning process resulted in well-defined goals and clear mission statements for the new unit.

One of their first decisions was to designate this unit as a lab, which, as the deputy director explained, was a way of tempering user expectations and presenting the project as a safe place for humanities scholars to tinker and experiment. Another important decision focused on providing the digital tools and services thought to be the most useful to the broadest possible spectrum of humanists. This strategy came directly from their goal to build a space that would bring DH into the mainstream rather than add to its ghettoization. The planning process also identified what the center would not do. The director clarified:

We were fairly careful to plan the lab to be as consistent with our mission and to do something that we thought was genuinely within the scope of our capacities. There were two things that we very consciously said we were not going to do. We decided we really wanted to make a research environment, and not a room full of hardware. So, the center is no place you can go and find lots of gadgets and play with wires. The second was that we understood that we did not have access to or the ability to manage and maintain archives. That, we realized, would be for the library.

As these examples show, planning a DH center is a complex task with many diverse components to consider and numerous stakeholders to consult. Equipping a center with the right personnel and technologies matters, as some authors point out (see Posner, 2013), but is insufficient to guarantee success.

Unlike more narrowly defined scholarly fields, DH has the potential to simultaneously support multiple lines of research. However, lack of direction when planning digital centers can leave this rich potential untapped. Without a strategically planned mission, DH centers could slip into amorphous units that serve everyone and no one. This is not to say that access to digital scholarship should in any way be prescribed or exclusive. The truth is that the financial, human, and technical resources of DH centers are limited, and putting them to the best use requires setting priorities and making certain trade-offs.

Important factors in planning DH centers include formulating goals and identifying the intended user community. These two strategies are closely intertwined but nonetheless difficult to execute. In a number of centers I visited, the main goal was to support humanities scholars in their current research and to gradually introduce them to digital tools and methods that might benefit their work. These centers target the widest possible spectrum of humanists as their potential user base rather than rely on scholars who were already well versed in, or inclined to use, digital tools. For example, a manager of one of the centers said their goal is to support researchers of all disciplines within the humanities, so they strive to provide digital research tools that are widely accessible and appealing to use. Another center I visited is also designed to attract the broadest spectrum of humanists, but for the purpose of facilitating collaborative work.[1] A third center set their mission in very sweeping terms, designing space and strategies to answer the question: "What could digital technologies do to help humanities?"

These centers bridge the critical gap between technologically advanced and less advanced scholars and promote an inclusive approach to DH. However, with wide-ranging goals and diverse user communities, these units sometimes struggle to identify and profile their activities. Humanists' interest in using digital technologies varies as much as their ability to do so. As I discussed in the previous chapters, addressing the differences among such a wide spectrum of proficiencies and scholarly needs is anything but straightforward.

For example, one center's planning process included surveying a large group of humanists, their potential users. The survey identified two distinct user types. One type included scholars who wanted digital tools and methods to help them search, communicate, and calendar more efficiently. The other identified group consisted of scholars interested in exploring how to use digital tools and methods to transform their research. With respect to these two user types, my interviewees concluded that if centers offered tools and services that were too complex, then scholars from the first group might try them once but get confused and not return to the center. Conversely, tools and services that are too simple could quickly become uninteresting to advanced users of the second group, who might then conclude the center did not suit their needs. "So, we tried to really strike the golden balance, and the way we tried to satisfy a wide variety of different users was just to make our tools and services very expandable and customizable," related one of the interviewees.

Some centers adopt a more prescribed approach when establishing goals and characterizing potential user communities. For instance, one of the centers I studied specifically targets graduate students as their primary users. They solicit applications from humanities graduate students in the process of writing their dissertations, award them stipends of $5,000–10,000, and then work with them, typically over the period of one year, to help the candidates complete their PhD projects. The projects they supported crossed a variety of disciplines, including English, French, history, anthropology, music, and economics. The upside for the center is that the applicants usually bring some experience with and enthusiasm for using digital tools. "These people tend to be pretty involved," explains the program director," and they help us push our own understanding of the methods. That's been a really positive system for us, because it helps build a community of early career scholars who are working with these tools." Community building is one of the strategic aims of this center, which is viewed as an investment in the local research community. The head of the R&D team observed that as students pursue training at the center, they talk to other students and, over time, help foster a community of young, technologically aware humanists.

The strategy of creating DH centers using very precisely defined goals and user communities sometimes stems from the financial need to position centers within the network of university research units. At one of the universities I visited, DH work spanned five separate academic sections: instructional technologies; digital research in the humanities, arts, and social sciences; digital experiential research; a digital library; and grant support. This complex organizational structure reflected the university's funding system. Specifically, the unit for instructional technologies was prohibited from supporting research projects because of the nature of its funding source. The director of this center explains:

> We are audited, and it's very carefully scrutinized, so we have to be very careful how we spend that money. Also, our instructional technology coordinator is fully paid by those fees, and he really can't focus on research projects.

Furthermore, this unit is part of the humanities division, and scholars from the social sciences are not able to apply for their support, even if working on DH projects. In response to his problem, a separate center for digital research in the humanities, arts, and social sciences emerged from the unit for instructional technologies. The head of this center explains:

> It's not their [Instructional Technologies'] mission to support social scientists, so anyone like that would come to our center; they have to bring their questions and their issues to us. It is an institutional problem.

The Digital Library Program at that university faces similar challenges. The Head of the Digital Library Program explained that they are affiliated with the humanities division and a separate library unit digitizes, stores, and provides access to data for the social sciences. Yet social scientists working on DH projects often store their materials and data in the humanities library unit. This convoluted setup causes duplication of effort and confusion among both researchers and librarians.

Interviewees at another research site cited this parallel functioning of disconnected DH centers as a significant problem on their campus as well. The DH units were differentiated according to the specific areas of work (instruction, research, etc.) that they support, and according to their funding sources. And while this organizational system can help research centers formulate clear goals and distinguish themselves, it can also lead to user confusion and other serious downsides: "They don't know which one's [center] the best for them and it may just turn them off from going anywhere. Or they'll just stick with what they know," the communication specialist at one of the centers concluded.

Outreach

Beyond formulating key goals and identifying an intended user-base, DH centers must also reach potential users. This outreach effort is particularly relevant, considering the misunderstandings and resistance toward digital scholarship sometimes held by traditionally trained humanists. As a case in point, one interviewee explained that a popular view among the humanists at his university sees DH as a passing trend and digital tools as something unusable for traditionally trained scholars. "And then they turn back and start e-mailing and going to Google Books," he said, adding, "There's a lot of people who rely on [digital] tools, but when they hear the word *digital humanities*, they don't think it's interesting to them."

My respondents thus point out that at DH centers, reaching out to potential users requires two crucial preparatory steps. The

Figure 4.1 Humanists rely on digital tools but fear digital humanities.

first is making humanists aware that they already rely on digital technologies, and thus, with more active involvement, they could positively shape the direction traditional and DH are heading. The second step involves creating the perception that DH centers are *offering* digital tools and methods to humanists rather than *imposing* them. For instance, the director at one of the centers said they detected considerable nervousness among potential users "about the way in which the DH might potentially mean the death of traditional humanities," so it was essential to first address those concerns before attempting to engage users in more advanced digital scholarship activities.

Scholars often have a fragmented understanding of how much research potential digital tools and methods actually hold. To increase awareness, DH centers adjust their outreach strategies and occasionally contact users one-on-one. My respondents at DH centers stressed that outreach needs to be personal in order to be successful. Therefore, they talk individually to potential users, explaining how digital tools and methods could be beneficial for specific research and teaching activities. This strategy also helps minimize potential misunderstandings and reduces scholars' anxiety. As my respondents pointed out, a problem arises when humanists think they are being brought in wholesale to a DH center just to be sold a software product, but not told the scholarly value of the product, that is, how it might help in their research practices. When this happens, the scholars quickly turn off. Talking to them one-to-one helps alleviate this problem and keeps the humanists engaged. Yet, this personal approach also has certain disadvantages. "There's nothing like the one-on-one explaining, talking, getting someone excited about something, but that's an obstacle because time is so precious, and everything seems like an extra, extra task," says a vice president of one the centers.

Indeed, outreach activities of DH centers frequently stumble upon the obstacle of their users having too little time and too few time management options. As discussed in chapter 3, scholars are predominantly concerned with publishing, teaching, and meeting administrative requirements. Finding time to acquire new digital skills poses a challenge that is often ignored. Interviewees at the DH centers I visited confirm this, stressing that they considered it an achievement just to be able to schedule time to talk with a humanities scholar. One of the interviewees told me:

> These are very busy people, and their concern is primarily what is their current research about and when can I make time for it. And very often they are ultimately making choices between do they go and pay attention to our offer of a demonstration about digital tools, or do they spend that hour and focus on their own research questions. And so, we're competing with natural priorities in a scholar's life.

Digital humanities centers also rely on word of mouth to reach potential users. Doing so enables them to apply a personalized user approach that synchs with how scholars most typically learn about digital tools and methods.[2] Furthermore, as discussed in chapter 3, scholars often believe that because only their peers understand epistemological and methodological complexity of particular research problems, they are the most credible sources for suggesting adequate digital tools and methods. Exchange of experiences among peers is thus one of the most successful outreach strategies:

> If you can reach the right people out in the faculty or even grad students sometimes, that's a much more compelling argument or case than anything that we can say. Even though we, ourselves, may have PhDs and may use technology for our own research, we're not in the same role as they are. So, hearing from someone who lives a life just like they do in many ways is very compelling. (Program director of the center)

Yet, not just needs on the user side dictate personalized outreach strategies. Several DH centers I studied maintain individualized approach to users as a way of coping with their own limited resources. They contact scholars individually because they need to walk the line between having enough people to work with and having too much work. "We can very quickly fall into a trap where we do not have the resources [to support all of the users]," said one of the interviewees, "so we are very cognizant of kind of slow block moves and very carefully picking who we are working with." This observation illustrates that, in addition to outreach, DH centers also need to develop strategies for providing continuous support to their users.

User Support

User support is an important, but not always clearly anticipated part of activities in DH centers. In the following example, a center failed to anticipate the staff and workload necessary to provide user support and maintain a user community:

> We just thought we were having fun, and the expectation was OK, we get that [the center] going, and they will come and use it. Well, no. You've got to be there with them for a while, watering the

flower every day so that it grows. I don't know what our expectation was, but that's been the biggest surprise. (Deputy director of the center)

"Watering the flower" means keeping regular office hours, organizing talks and workshops, answering user inquiries, and similar support activities. Growing useful and well-used DH centers also involves balancing various disciplines within the user community so that no single discipline dominates the center's activities and conversations.[3] Finally, an important element of maintaining user communities involves shaping user expectations.

Unlike commercial services, or even university-sponsored technical support, DH centers are research units with activities distributed across diverse segments of practice. This means that they cannot always respond instantaneously to user requests, an increasingly common expectation in the technology-driven culture of immediacy (see Anderson and Rainie, 2012). According to my respondents, scholars typically complain if they do not have prompt and convenient access to research materials or services. As a codirector of one of the centers put it, "The main challenge is tempering expectations, because sometimes we deal with faculty members that want an enormous amount of things finished as soon as possible."

In addition to adjusting user expectations about the availability of support, DH centers must also clarify the nature of their partnership with users. One of the commonly held misconceptions about DH centers is that users view them as existing solely to answer humanists' requests rather than to collaborate with them. An employee at one of the centers elaborated:

Sometimes, there's kind of a clash between where they [humanities faculty] see their role and where they see our role; they see us as the programming shop that will do whatever they tell us to, and that's not really how we're trying to approach this. It's more of collaboration, and we actually get something back out of it also.

This false perception can also arise from how DH centers are organized and classified within the university. Too often, universities position and treat DH centers as service-orientated facilities instead of as research units (see Fraistat, 2012).

Hybrids at Work

The institutional and financial constraints profiled in the previous section often mean that DH centers cannot afford a permanent staff of dedicated computer scientists or developers. Instead, technical expertise comes from occasional partnerships with university IT departments or—more frequently—from employing traditionally trained humanists who also have good computer skills, and who are sometimes designated as "hybrids."[4]

These personnel are seen as a necessary link between "the two cultures," as they can understand the needs and values of both cultures, and adeptly translate epistemological and methodological concepts and approaches. "Smart organizations will have more of me," remarked the head of the R&D team at one of the DH centers who also happens to be a historian with good programming skills. The advantage of speaking both "programese" and "scholarese," as this interviewee put it, is the capacity to help humanists grasp digital tools and methods while simultaneously helping programmers understand humanities work. Recalling a conversation with his friend, a programmer at Google conceded that while humanities scholars ask very interesting questions, their questions are not always interesting to programmers:

> That kind of stuck with me, because a lot of times you've got to rephrase a project and make it interesting to the individual programmer, so they're not just sitting there writing code that somebody else is going to use. If you have a humanities center, you need somebody who can talk and motivate people in the programming side and actually explain what a humanist is talking about.

Digital humanities centers have found an efficient way of employing "hybrids" through engaging humanities graduate students in their activities. Graduate students often work as tutors in those centers, introducing scholars to digital technologies, in what might be seen as a specific reversal of instructional positions and hierarchies. As my respondents commented, this arrangement succeeds because graduate students are usually early adopters of technology who immediately assess new digital tools and enthusiastically pass along those they like. Engaging them in this hybrid role is a win-win—the faculty receive necessary technology support and the graduate students sharpen their skillsets to be better instructors.

Indeed, graduate students with whom I talked liked working in DH research centers. It allowed them to advance their research skills while gaining access to various digital resources and tools. At the same time, these jobs enabled them to build professional experience and expertise through participation in important research and decision-making activities concerning implementation of DH services. Finally, the reversal of instructional roles, in which students were teaching teachers, facilitated the students' understanding of some of the didactic principles motivating them to develop their own pedagogic strategies. For instance, one of the graduate students described his work with the faculty in this manner:

> You're doing work with people who are the smartest people on the earth in their particular discipline. On average, they don't like to admit that they don't know something. When someone comes up with a new idea, especially a lowly grad student, a lot of time the faculty will stick to the way they've done it. So, it's not trying to force things upon them, but it's trying to present things in the same way that you would pedagogically teach a difficult concept. If I can present it in such a way that leads them to discovering on their own, they have a sense of ownership of the idea, so that's "teaching the old dog new tricks," if I can say that.

Alternative Academic Careers

The idea of hybrids as a type of scholarly workforce can be closely linked to the concept of alternative academic careers. In the DH field, an alternative career path usually refers to traditionally trained humanists, typically a PhD, who steps off the tenure track for an academic position "requiring deep understanding of humanities scholarship, but outside of the ranks of the tenured or tenure-track teaching faculty" (Nowviskie, 2011: 7).

Scholars in alternative academic careers hold positions of university staff, library or nontenure track faculty, consultants, or managers. Others work as employees or contractors at universities, museums, archives, libraries, and other institutions (see Nowviskie, 2011). Fraistat (2012) posits that because DH centers are "increasingly being staffed by a new kind of hybrid scholar with advanced degrees in the humanities and their own research agendas" (p. 289), this shift is helping to update old perceptions about faculty and staff positions as being research versus service roles.

My interviewees described alternative academic paths as intentional career choices scholars make. For instance, some of the academics gave up tenured faculty jobs in favor of staff positions at DH centers. Although this choice allows scholars to continue working in their preferred field the transition is nonetheless perceived as difficult and consequential: "You can't just yank somebody out of the faculty and out of years or decades of training without some accounting for how they conceive of themselves as a scholar," one of the respondents remarked. This readjustment becomes particularly challenging given a tendency to label nontenure track PhDs as "failed academics." In essence, practitioners who pursue alternative academic careers risk professional setbacks if their skills and positions are still evaluated within the traditional tenure paradigms they left. One of the interviewees, a director of a DH center, described the dilemma:

> From an administrative point of view, or theoretical point of view, how are we thinking about people's time and labor? It's going to be maybe *the* issue that I think [digital humanities] centers should engage with in some way, because our internal inherited systems of classifying employees are not well suited [to digital humanities practices]." (Emphasis in the original)

Heads of DH centers with whom I talked see this issue as an important concern in their work. They explain that they work as hard as they can, within the regulations that they inherited, to achieve the same status and recognition for alternative academics as those afforded their tenure-track colleagues.

Traditional organizational systems for classifying scholars are not only inefficient for addressing contemporary issues of academic labor and knowledge production, they are also potentially detrimental to the future of scholarly work. One of the interviewees summarized those fears:

> If we can't get this generation of graduate students comfortable with alternate modes of work, not feeling like they are failures if they don't get a tenure-track position, and seeing good career paths for themselves within the digital humanities, we're going to lose that generation of scholars. (Director of the center)

An important aspect of hybrids' work at DH centers involves developing digital research tools and projects. In this context, the debate between generic versus boutique tools, discussed in chapter 3, resurfaces. In the past, DH centers tended to invest their scarce resources into building specialized tools, which only worked on specific projects. Contemporary centers support more generic tool building. From the centers' point of view, generic tools have the advantage of greater external and internal funding and administrative support. My respondents emphasized that it is easier for them to persuade a funding agency or university to invest in a generic tool that can potentially be repurposed and reused within the university or the academy than it is to ask for money to develop a task-specific, boutique tool.

Openness and interoperability of generic tools are also valued features. Converting home-built tools into open source, interoperable systems, however, can be challenging for DH centers. "We have to be much more flexible, so we are changing from much more monolithic structures to structures that can integrate easily with a lot of other systems," one of the interviewees explained.

Many respondents agreed that DH centers need to be more systematic in how they address the entire process of tool and project development. They identified the "start-up mentality" as a particular weakness among current initiatives, believing this approach favors the new idea over the importance of a creating a sustainable, development cycle. Citing open source communities as a benchmark, the respondents suggested that adopting practices such as documenting the entire tool development process and performing regular usability testing would contribute to building better tools in DH.

Some respondents also took note of the double bind inherent to building academic tools, that is, finding the necessary resources to maintain, update, and support the tool as the user base increases. They pointed out that it is hard enough to motivate scholars to use these tools, but the problem worsens when centers cannot support successful uptake. As one of the interviewees offered:

> Most digital humanities centers do not have that capacity, and so we both want to be software development shops and not be industry. But industry really knows how to do the lifecycle [of a tool], and we generally don't, and we don't have the resources to do it. So, almost everything gets back to a loop where you're in a kind of a double bind.

Benefits and Challenges

The field of DH still lacks recognition among traditional humanities departments and programs, as discussed in chapter 3. Hence, DH centers are frequently the first, and sometimes only, encounter that humanists have with the field. Furthermore, employees at DH centers are often the only ones who work with humanists on both theoretical and hands-on aspects of their engagement with digital tools and methods. Therefore, it is useful to understand what employees of DH centers think of as the key benefits and central challenges of their work specifically, and of DH in general.

When considering the benefits of DH, respondents differentiated between short-term and long-term benefits. The most common short-term benefits they identified were ease and speed of completing certain scholarly tasks and broad access to research materials. In that sense, these interviewees concurred with the majority of humanities respondents. However, when asked about long-term benefits, scholars working in DH centers had insights into more sophisticated, less obvious rewards of digital scholarship, compared to the majority of mainstream humanists.

Figure 4.2 Comparing benefits and challenges.

The chief long-term benefits that respondents identified pertain to knowledge production in the humanities, exemplified in transformed practices and values that humanists apply to their work. An often-cited benefit is collaboration, seen as the potential for humanists to connect with colleagues engaged in similar research projects, to respond faster to research questions, and to create a different paradigm for how humanists conduct research.

The collaborative aspect of DH is also credited with opening up the early developmental stages of humanists' work. Humanists are typically reluctant to present and disseminate their work until it is in final stages and near completion. Therefore, one of the perceived long-term benefits of DH is that humanists may get accustomed to sharing in-progress work at various research stages. My respondents reported seeing this shift in action:

> I'm watching this process unfold where scholars who have been trained to work in solitary ways are now suddenly finding

themselves collaborating and sharing with large groups, and I'm fascinated by the ways in which that's enriching and causing research in the digital humanities just to blossom. (Head of R&D at a DH center)

A related long-term benefit that my respondents saw is the transformation and expansion of the scope of humanists' epistemological and methodological assumptions. Digital humanities work is seen as bringing a new way of looking at old humanities questions and as provoking humanists to ask the kind of questions they could not ask before. One of the most important manifestations of this transformation is humanists' relationship with empirical components (as detailed in chapter 3) and in particular with their epistemic perception of data:

> Humanists are very new to the idea of "I work with data?" Well, of course. Every poem you are working with is data, but we haven't been trained to think in those ways. So, I think that one benefit might be a reorientation of our ideas about what we do as humanists, what constitutes knowledge. I think the benefit could be that it allows us to have new insights that arise any time you get a shake-up of perspective. (Director of a DH center)

This advice, however, is not just the naïve yielding to the empirical and quantitative. Rather it demonstrates how significantly the humanists' interpretative approach to data can contribute to contemporary scholarship. Such an approach renews the question of digitization versus analysis, which has been haunting the field of DH for decades:

> You can't just stop at digitizing books and having that data available and being able to search them. It's putting together the questions, and really thinking about what are the larger questions that we can now answer having this data, how can we interpret it in ways that shed light on the kinds of questions that humanities scholars ask. (Professor of literary studies and a codirector of a DH center)

The long-term benefits of DH that my respondents discussed derive in part from the major challenges they face in their own work, and in part from the general field of DH. One of the biggest obstacles that they singled out is that humanists' seem to prefer to work individually. These proprietary tendencies inhibit scholarly collaboration and restrict cooperative development of generic research tools. The respondents emphasized that while humanists are used to working alone, a successful technology exploration or DH project requires collaboration, particularly because it is still rare to find a humanist who is proficient at both programming and humanistic inquiry. Not surprisingly, overcoming this legacy of mistrust among humanists is more than a challenge; it is a prerequisite for successful development of digital research tools.

With respect to tool development, my respondents view humanists' lack of influence on the process as a substantial problem (examined in chapter 3), attributed predominantly to a culture gap:

> I don't think it [the gap] is at the very technical level. In terms of thinking about organizations, thinking at the very high level that would direct development—we see huge language and culture gaps. So, any ways those can be bridged will help humanists to say what kinds of tools would be of use. (Professor of Spanish and a director of a DH center)

The larger consequence of the current (non)collaborative environment in DH is its self-perpetuating nature in that it motivates people to situate their scholarship in very specific, limiting ways. Digital humanities projects, however, if suitably planned and executed, could slowly change humanists' insular attitude toward the purpose of their work. In discussing how to change this mindset, my respondents commented further that these attitudes reflect economic circumstances and the overarching academic structure of tenure and career advancement in the humanities. When evaluating new research practices, scholars want to know how these novelties affect their ability to advance in the increasingly frightening world of fewer jobs and reduced funding. Therefore, among the changes necessary to encourage collaboration and uptake of digital tools and methods is a significant shift in the reward system, and the prestige attached to certain types of scholarly engagement and publications:

> Maybe the component of being able to collaborate can be a measure by which one gets tenure. If someone is a really excellent collaborator, and they generate projects with other people, that's something that should be valued. Currently, it's not really valued except maybe collegiality, which doesn't get you a whole lot.

Another important adjustment would be incentivizing humanists to schedule time to learn digital tools and methods. Repeatedly, my respondents mentioned scholars' lack of time, and stressed that humanists will adopt digital tools and methods if they are useful to their work and careers Therefore, incentivizing humanists through recognized scholarly rewards could be very effective:

> If there were academic credit assigned, then people would automatically choose to set aside time or look for ways to get time released so that they could do this in some way. And that would make a world of difference in the outcome. (Head of a DH center)

Another strategy to encourage technology adoption is inspiring and encouraging humanists to become more flexible with regard to how they define their particular discipline and work style. "So often, people will choose the harder path, but the path that they know. And it's hard to break people from that," one of the interviewees concluded. Similarly, the respondents agreed that it is very hard to teach people to do something different from what they are used to doing, as well as to train people to do things that they do not want to do. At the same time, they argue that humanists, if not pushed in new directions, will yield to inertia:

> And that's something that we deal with here. We want to push the boundaries of what humanities research is and the digital humanities methods, but we have to do it in a way that makes sense to people who have never worked in those methods.

Part of the resistance is that traditionally trained humanists rarely have formal technology training or even an affinity for the field. "It's viewed as almost contradictory; if you focus on technology, you can't be a humanities person, the two don't necessarily mix," noted one of the interviewees. Therefore, a conceptual gap that needs to be addressed concerns the value capacity in DH, as discussed in chapter 3. An important component of this conversation for both trainees and educators is recognizing that the transition is more than mechanical. It is a fundamental shift. When humanists start dealing with quantitative data and methods, it changes the way they write, the venues where they choose to publish, and many other academic-driven decisions. Internal disciplinary conflicts arise when conclusions are reached through novel methods, such as drawing a statistical inference about a corpus of text. My respondents further suggest that humanists sometimes define themselves in the negative space of the sciences, which adds to these conflicts.

The role DH centers play in breaking down these complexities of shifting epistemic practices and commitments is considerable. One part of the task is familiarizing humanists with the epistemological and methodological elements of the transition. Another component depends on making the shift manageable to grasp and adopt:

> And I think we've been able to break that down into smaller steps that people can make without dumbing it down, without making it seem trivial, but really emphasizing the real shift in thinking that's happening in the humanities, and supporting that with the technical side. I think what really excites faculty is the abstract and the intellectual challenge of research, and the way that reorients and changes the way they think about their discipline. It's a huge institutional change and a generational change, but I think that argument is gaining support.

Finally, another serious barrier that the respondents identified specifically in their own work and generally across the humanities is the narrow disciplinary scope and textual focus of the field, as discussed in chapter 1. Various interviewees posited that mainly literary scholars and historians run the field of DH, and, as an outcome, a good number of humanities disciplines get overlooked in a DH discussion. An additional consequence of such a situation is favoring text-based projects and Text Encoding Initiative (TEI) over other streams of work in DH. My respondents countered this preference by emphasizing the importance of accepting methodological diversity in the DH enterprise and the need to hear from those humanities disciplines lacking a voice in the current DH discussion.

Future

Organizational changes discussed in this chapter arise as both an answer and an impetus to a web of transformations in contemporary scholarly practice. Therefore, it is important to understand what is the vision of DH that organizational changes articulated through DH centers imply, and in what ways the imagining of DH as theory and practice might shape future institutional changes in academia.

Among my respondents, two related but disparate theories of the future of DH emerged. One line of thinking suggested that scholarly transformations necessitate gradual and organic development and that the use of digital tools and methods will progressively become a standard part of humanities research practices. The premise of this approach is this: what we identify as innovative DH methods today will become traditional, established humanities methods in the future. Different avenues will lead us to the mainstream acceptance of digital methods, especially as DH become more engrained in the classroom.

This approach further holds that organizational transfigurations implemented through top-down initiatives and funding bolsters can foster certain aspects of scholarly change, but that they can neither replace nor accelerate reflexivity of the learning process that both individuals and disciplines experience when encountering new methods and forms of knowledge production. Accordingly, my respondents advocated for the "slow time" of DH, cautioning that change does not happen overnight. Similarly, they advocate for the "silent time" of DH, suggesting that humanists' critiques and doubts toward digital tools and methods do not necessarily need to be discussed publicly:

> Just keep it to ourselves. Otherwise, you ferment this notion of humanists as being flaky and not capable. We're extremely capable. We just have to gain some literacy in areas that we haven't had before. (Deputy director at a DH center)

Scholars who subscribe to this line of thought further suggest that DH should be marked as a transitional moment in the humanities disciplines rather than as a distinct field of scholarly practice. They reason that the term "digital humanities" will likely disappear as the distinction between digital and mainstream humanities diminishes over time, even though certain methodological differences might remain:

> Those groups that have methodological differences will still bifurcate, will still stay somewhat separate, but I think that's true of a non-digital fashion, too. But, there are certain other things where it's really going to blend, and you're not going to know whether it's digital or not. (Professor of English and head of an international DH association)

By contrast, another group of my respondents held that DH already ranks as a distinct field. They also believe the field will retain its autonomy because the need for innovative work and thinking with technology in the humanities will never cease. For instance, a director of one of the DH centers says he is not persuaded by the argument that the distinction between digital and mainstream humanities will disappear, as it presumes a teleological approach:

> We get to a certain point, and technology is already doing everything we could ever want or imagine, so why need the people who innovate? But I think there will always be a need for people who are innovating, bringing new forms and understandings of technology.

Similarly, a director of another center posits that although the use of digital tools and methods will become increasingly mainstream, there will always be a need for research groups on the frontier of innovation: "Saying that it will all just get mainstreamed and it will fade into the woodwork is really short-sighted, in my mind," she argued.

This debate about the future of DH is framed around two related questions. The first question is whether "digital shift" represents a means that moves humanities disciplines from point A (traditional humanities) to point B (DH), or is it a constantly unfolding process in which only provisional markers and phases of development can be identified. The second question is whether "digital shift" represents a change that transcends humanities practices of knowledge production in such a way that it needs to be articulated as a distinct field, or is it a transition of and within the existing humanities disciplines. The responses to these positions are as much in dispute as the underlying questions.

Both supporters and detractors of DH as a stand-alone field take somewhat ambiguous positions in that regard. On the one hand, each camp insists on digital scholarship being embraced by traditional disciplines and evaluated within the established cannons of humanities knowledge production. On the other hand, they advocate for universities and funding bodies to treat digital scholarship autonomously when it comes to managing organizational units, faculty, staff, students, projects, academic rewards, and funding. Such an ambiguous attitude can be seen as an element of the diffusion of innovation, but it can also be reflective of a broader structure of academic institutions. Persuasive work of knowledge production plays an important role in academic functioning (see Antonijević et al., 2013), and also shapes current and future forms of DH. My respondents saw this debate as a political and rhetorical trait of DH. One of the respondents articulated this stance in the following way:

> That [future of digital humanities] is a political question. That doesn't have anything to do with how we do our research. It has to do with institutional politics and disciplinary politics. I think it is a twofold question: how do we see ourselves as humanists in 20 years, and then how do our institutions change. The second one is definitely very political. And I know how I would

approach it politically; we need to start getting the big money so that we can insert our agenda into the larger IT planning. (Co-director of a DH center)

Funding and positioning of DH centers within the university organizational infrastructures play a compelling role, as discussed in chapter 1, and my respondents expected that fiscal and organizational matters will continue to determine the future fate of these centers and DH in general:

Economies are bad, budgets are getting cut at universities, and people are going to come to you and ask how do you justify your center's existence, what have you done that's mattered for scholars? And if you can't answer that, you'll get shut down. (Director of a DH center)

Questions around academic positioning and resource allocation also fuel debates about a separate field versus a stream of scholarship within the humanities discipline. Like scholars, university administrators are also musing about whether specialized DH centers will be needed in the future or if digital scholarship will blend into the existing disciplinary and departmental structures. The far-reaching presumably rhetorical question of whether technologically enabled scholarship will be designated as DH or "just" humanities will have important implications for the future of that kind of work, and humanities in general. As one of the respondents put it: "It may wind up for places like this to get written into strategic plans for universities and disappear, unless we rethink our vocabulary about this [digital humanities] work." Overall, my respondents agreed that we will see a wave of interest in DH centers and labs, some of which will persist and others of which will peak quickly only to fade away.

In such transitional moments, it is important to understand the disciplinary boundaries and organizational conflicts, which specify where the domain of traditional humanities ends and the domain of DH begins; to what extent do these domains overlap; and how disciplinary conflicts arise and get resolved. The domain of DH is not an exception in that regard. Articulation of new scholarly phenomena commonly arises out of confrontation between competing epistemologies, knowledge claims, and knowledge authorities and their attempts to reorganize both theory and practice of knowledge production (see Jasanoff, 2004). An array of discussions, reconfigurations, and negotiations arise within existing knowledge domains during times of epistemic and methodological shifts and conflicts. Therefore, stances taken by different stakeholders concerning the current and future status of DH are not straightforward epistemic and/or methodological attitudes. Instead they are positions built on a myriad of variables such as a stakeholder's position in the academic hierarchy, the level of standardization of DH research practices in an institution, and many other factors.

Examining this complex web of relations, this chapter encompassed the study's empirical framework. The following and final chapter aligns these transformations side-by-side to examine areas of confluence and divergence through analytical frameworks of boundary work and socio-technical expectations.

CHAPTER 5

Beyond Expectations

Describing the process of planning the Bamboo Project humanities cyberinfrastructure,[1] Dombrowski (2014) specified that this project was expected to

Implement a robust, scalable web services framework and a set of services that aligned with scholarly practice in the humanities, as defined by participating scholars. *In reality, this plan changed dramatically when faced with the interests and priorities of actual humanities scholars.* (p. 3; italics added)

Four years and $1.3 million dollars later, this project was quietly discontinued, failing to meet some of its main goals and expectations (ibid.). The project went astray despite the large budget, detailed planning, and involvement of two hundred participants from 75 renowned institutions. Although each unhappy digital humanities project is unhappy in its own way, to paraphrase Tolstoy, the Bamboo example is still instructive in demonstrating the complexity that underlies a broad set of transformations arising from the encounters between digital technologies and humanities.

The theoretical narratives and empirical results of this study charted such complex transformations in humanities scholarship at the individual, disciplinary, and organizational levels, illustrating internal and external dynamics in the humanities disciplines and in digital humanities. The narratives highlighted several themes significant for contemporary and future encounters of the humanities with digital technologies, telling the interconnected stories of practices, expectations, and fears. These practices, expectations, and fears also operate in narrative terms, shaping the visions and directions of humanities knowledge production in the digital age.

As discussed in chapter 1, the term "digital humanities" came to prominence in the early 2000s as an updated designator for the field of humanities computing, and also as a tactical term aimed at positioning digital humanities within institutional, financial, and disciplinary structures of contemporary academia. Over the past ten years, this term has been increasingly used as an overreaching designator of humanists' engagement with digital technologies. One root of this generalization was a lethargic response from the broader humanities community to digital scholarship. Another root emerged from the efforts of the digital humanities community to establish itself as the leader of digital knowledge production in the humanities. This community aspired to "play an inaugural role" in the humanities' encounter with digital scholarship, maintaining that it held "the potential to use new technologies to help the humanities communicate with, and adapt to, contemporary society" (see 4Humanities, Mission).

Digital humanities thus started to serve both as a designator of "a field with a discernable set of academic lineages, practices, and methodologies and a vague umbrella term used to describe the application of digital technology to traditional humanistic inquiry" (Gold, 2012: 68). This discursive ambiguity might seem insignificant or even constructive, as Kirschenbaum (2012) argued, but it also points to deeper and more consequential discrepancies about digital knowledge production in the humanities.

This chapter focuses on these discrepancies and suggests potential resolutions. I begin by looking at how boundary work—the discursive and practice-based processes of demarcating authorized knowledge, institutions, and practitioners from other intellectual activities and actors (see Gieryn, 1983; Bowker and Star, 1999; Carlile, 2002)—unfolds in the field of digital humanities. Based on this discussion, I propose an analytical distinction between digital humanities and digital scholarship in the humanities. Next, I examine expectations surrounding digital knowledge production in the humanities, together with evaluative and organizational possibilities for addressing those expectations. I end the chapter, and this book, with a call for a pluralistic future of digital knowledge production in the humanities.

Boundaries and Practices

An important element of narratives about digital humanities spotlights boundaries, specifically what type of humanists' engagement with digital tools and methods constitutes digital humanities work, and what type of humanists' interaction with digital technologies lies outside the scope of the field. Such attempts at categorizing scholars and their activities still influence discussions in the digital humanities, as I discussed in chapter 1. Raley (2014) refers to this boundary work arguing that, "once out of the 'wilderness that was humanities computing' and given a new title, the digital humanities became available to competing claims for intellectual and institutional territory" (p. 1). These territories and borders are charted in different ways, but mostly through negative identification as to what *does not* constitute digital humanities work. Ramsay (2011) posits that scholars' use of technology that excludes making or building falls outside the boundaries of digital humanities. Burdick and colleagues (2012) describe even narrower boundaries, excluding "the mere use of digital tools for the purpose of humanistic research and communication" (p. 122). The same approach is evident in Fitzpatrick's (2012) rhetorical question: Should the floodgates of digital humanities be opened so widely as "to include . . . 'every medievalist with a website,'" followed by her categorical response: "Undoubtedly not" (p. 14).

These and similar efforts to structure knowledge comprise an integral part of academic fields as the sites of struggle for determining criteria of legitimate membership and hierarchy (Bourdieu, 1988). The debates of legitimacy correspond to the related struggle for resource allocation. Alavarado (2011) thus accurately observes that digital humanities' boundary work burgeons with the field's growth in size and popularity, creating "the emergence of a territorial instinct in an environment of scarce resources" (para. 2).

Yet, boundaries of a scholarly field are social constructs that do not result from an assumed disciplinary reality; instead, they generate and structure that reality. The boundaries of a field do not inevitably correspond to knowledge production in practice, that is, to specific ways in which disciplinary knowledge is structured, employed, and reconstructed in scholars' everyday work. Only empirical investigation of practice can reveal boundaries of a field, because these boundaries emerge where the effects of the field end (see Wacquant, 1989: 39).

The challenge of determining where the effects of digital humanities cease is significant. At the core of this problem are two interrelated matters. One is the ubiquitous role of digital technologies in the work of contemporary humanists, who are often ambiguously labeled as "mainstream" humanists. The second is a continuing struggle within the field of digital humanities to position itself as a big "tent" supporting humanists' encounters with digital technologies, albeit with the Orwellian twist that some of those encounters are more equal than others.

To better understand this debate, let us return to Fitzpatrick's work. In the same text quoted above, Fitzpatrick proposed that digital humanities be understood as "a nexus of fields within which scholars use computing technologies to investigate the kinds of questions that are traditional to the humanities" (p. 12). Following this broad definition, she nonetheless argued that the definition of the field should not be expanded as much as to include *all* instances of humanists' engagement with digital technologies. The author did not specify which types of humanists' engagement with digital technology remain outside the field, but postulated instead that "there are scholars who work with digital materials but who remain outside the traditions and assumptions of the digital humanities" (p. 14).

Fitzpatrick's ambiguity in defining digital humanities is far from unique. In fact, the entire field faces the same trouble of explaining that it, somehow, simultaneously includes and excludes humanities research in and with digital technologies. In a curious way, the field that can agree neither on its definition and scope, nor on a clear criteria for evaluating its disciplinary content (even knowing whether or not a project is finished)[2] seems to feel comfortable and confident assessing whether someone is or is not a digital humanist. Additionally curious is the internal debate as to what exactly transforms a "mainstream" humanist into a "digital" one. Sometimes, it is the ability to code, other times the propensity to build (Ramsay, 2011); on the list are also "the core competencies" a digital humanist should possess (Burdick et al., 2012), as well as an endorsement of the traditions and assumptions of digital humanities (Fitzpatrick, 2012). Essentially, it appears a scholar needs the seal of approval from those already initiated in the digital humanities community. This dynamics appears as a reversal of the process discussed in chapters 3 and 4, in which humanists' digital work gets excluded from "humanities proper," forcing scholars to switch to alternative career tracks or to double their efforts by producing both "tenurable" and innovative work.

This type of boundary work is not unique to digital or mainstream humanities. For instance, almost identical paths to designing a new field of expertise and an exclusive expert profile characterized electrical engineering in the late nineteenth century. An emerging field at that time, electrical engineering suffered the same professional anxieties we see in the digital humanities today. The field struggled to position itself on equal footing with other areas of specialization and to attain a recognized, preferably elite status in the society (see Marvin, 1988). To that end, it was important to establish well-defined boundaries of the field, which "by the time of its organization had achieved no clear consensus about the meaning of the term *electrical engineer*" (ibid., p. 10; italics in the original). Like in contemporary digital humanities, the essential element of boundary work included determining who was *in* and who was *out* of the field, that is, who had a legitimate right to assume the title of an expert. Marvin explains that much of the activity and literature in early electrical engineering "was occupied with sorting and labeling insiders and outsiders," while the field's frontrunners "were wont to indulge a powerful impulse to identify aliens...defined as those who were uneasy and unfamiliar with technical procedures and attitudes" (p. 15). Such more than a century-old premises about expertise are strikingly reminiscent to those formulated in contemporary digital humanities, where a set of predominantly technical competencies is presumed to define an expert, while assumptions outside the field's *doxa* characterizes an outsider.

Boundary work and definitional deadlocks in digital humanities are particularly relevant today when humanists' engagement with technologies increasingly becomes the "new normal" (see Brown et al., 2006; Meyer et al., 2009; Wyatt and Millen, 2014). As Chun and Rhody (2014) put it, "Unless there is a core contingent of faculty who continue to distribute their work in typed manuscripts and consult print indexes of periodicals... everyone is already a digital humanist insofar as it is *a condition of contemporary research*" (p. 9; italics added). However, this fact is often obscured through boundary work in digital humanities that sets "digital" and "mainstream" humanities apart, as well as through the focus on big data and complex computational methods in broader discussions of digital scholarship. Such a focus creates a perception that research in the sciences would be impossible without digital technologies, while humanities could get along fine without it. By contrast, my study demonstrates that the work of contemporary humanists would be fundamentally different, if not impossible, without digital technologies. This applies to both scholars who use basic digital techniques, such as accessing research materials at remote sites, as well as to those who utilize complex computational modeling. Digital technologies permeate all phases of humanists' workflow to varying degrees of adoption and impact, as I discussed in chapter 3, reaffirming Wyatt and Millen's argument that "all [humanities] research and scholarship has already been changed by the widespread availability of digital tools" (2014, p. 11).

Humanities scholarship, even the "mainstream" one, already follows the route of digital scholarship as a condition of contemporary research. A full transition in that direction is both inevitable and necessary. However, the question that needs further discussion is what that "full transition" means, to whom, and what parallel paths it could take. Additional question is whether the field of digital humanities represents the best route of that transition. While discourses surrounding digital humanities assert expectations about revolutionizing and/or saving humanities (see 4Humanities, Mission), studies suggest that this field still resides on the margins of humanities scholarship (see Juola, 2008; Thaller, 2012). At the same time, digital technologies have become prevalent in humanists' daily practices, revealing an evolution of humanities scholarship that has been slowly unfolding in the background, transforming humanists' research and teaching practices (see Liu, 2009). But, as Brown and colleagues (2003) warn:

> We tend to "cite" people making a promise or deploying a futuristic image. The side effect of this is that we become less analytically sensitive to the expression of expectations that are not accompanied by obvious speech-acts. . . . There might be routines or other temporalities in which a future is embedded whilst not necessarily being articulated in language, metaphor or discourse per se. (p. 8)

Indeed, numerous humanities scholars have been actively interacting with digital tools and methods in their research and teaching practices without articulating that engagement through the digital humanities discourse. As described in chapters 2 and 3, humanists' uptake of digital tools and methods often emerges spontaneously, based on a specific scholarly need or from practical research and teaching demands. Once so adopted, digital technologies continue to interact with scholars' workflows quietly, often escaping their own attention[3] and remaining outside the dominant digital humanities discussion. As Wouters and Beaulieu (2006) observe, the aspirations of establishing new paradigms of digital knowledge production often unfold in tension with actual research practices, silencing various scholarly voices along the way.

Ultimately, those scholars and their work need a voice in the humanities transition toward digital scholarship. I am not referring primarily to the understated economic, political, or cultural issues in the digital humanities—such as ethnocentrism, gender issues, or funding imbalance—which are discussed in chapter 1, and which are also highly important. I am arguing for a much closer attention to the variety of unrecognized scholarly practices

Figure 5.1 The transition toward digital scholarship.

and achievements in humanists' engagement with digital technologies that fall outside the existing purview of digital humanities.

Focusing on this diversity of scholarly voices is necessary because neither the boundaries nor the complexity of the humanities engagement with digital scholarship can be grasped unless we look beyond the image of a "digital humanist" as currently construed in digital humanities. Digital knowledge production in the humanities cannot be reduced to a singular focus, that one of the digital humanities, not because this field is an a-theoretical, money-grabbing monster, as some critiques charge,[4] but because socio-technical, epistemological, and methodological reality of digital knowledge production in the humanities is much broader than any one field or "tent." Therefore, *disentangling* digital humanities and digital scholarship in the humanities could be a useful distinction for analytical and pragmatic purposes.

Digital Humanities and Digital Scholarship in the Humanities

While digital humanists may not want to know "what is" digital humanities and such ambivalence might be useful to them, as Kirschenbaum (2014) argued, it is not constructive for humanities scholarship. To start with, digital humanities is a very broad term. Taken literally, it refers to all humanists who engage with digital technologies in their scholarly practice, even the "medievalist with a website" Fitzpatrick described. Yet, boundary work of differentiating between accepted and unaccepted practices constantly reappears in the digital humanities, communicating who is *in* and who is *out* of the field. Such an approach, again, is not unique to digital humanities. For instance, Craig (1999) describes the development of communication studies, where a broad designator *communication* was used as an "institutional legitimizing device in ways that precluded any coherent definition of the field" (p. 122). Through the use of such a broad and vague designator, the field claimed authority over a vast set of approaches, practices, concepts, and areas of study, becoming "an intellectual Taiwan" that "claim[ed] to be all of China when, in act, it was isolated on a small island" (Peters, cited in Craig, p. 122).

The field of digital humanities can similarly be seen as "an intellectual Taiwan claiming to be all of China." My study and the body of other authors' works demonstrate that the diversity in humanists' engagement with digital technologies exceeds the existing boundaries of digital humanities. If the field that has self-adopted a broad designator of digital humanities is unable or unwilling to embrace a diversity that both this term and humanists' practices entail, than either it needs to switch to yet another in a long history of its designators, or some of the constituents upon which it claims discursive authority might need to distance themselves from that field. It is unsustainable that digital humanities claims and manages institutional and financial support over the entire humanities engagement with digital technologies, yet acts as arbitrator of the "appropriate" forms and methods of that engagement. Furthermore, as I have cited throughout this book, the field of digital humanities struggles with deep, persistent disagreements about its fundamental epistemological and methodological scope, directions, and commitments. It is unwarranted to transfer this field's inner tensions and controversies to humanities scholarship in general. It would be more constructive to move beyond the debate about "digital" versus "mainstream" humanities toward differentiating between digital humanities and digital scholarship in the humanities.

My conceptualization of digital scholarship in the humanities draws on Jankowski's (2009) definition of e-Research, as well as on Wouters and Beaulieu's (2006) argument for conceiving of digital scholarship beyond computation. Digital scholarship in the humanities can be conceptualized as humanities scholarly activities carried out with the use of digital tools, resources, and methods across the spectrum of computational complexity. It encompasses both high-performance and low-performance computational tools and methods ranging from digital "primitives," such as electronic search or blogging, to complex computational modeling. Regardless of the level of computational complexity, digital scholarship in the humanities prompts changes in the ways humanists envision, carry out, communicate, and organize their work and approach their objects of inquiry. Instead of provisionary classifications, transformations in the ways of knowing define the boundaries of digital knowledge production in the humanities.

To illustrate this, let me return to an example of an assistant professor of comparative literature, described in chapter 4. His most recent project, a collaborative book translation with a colleague in Japan, was completed through Google Docs. By jointly composing and editing translations in Google Docs, they reached the point of collaboration in which they did not know who translated what. This process, in their view, resulted in a much better final output than doing it "the old way." These scholars do not identify with the digital humanities community, nor is it likely that this community would recognize their work as digital humanities. Their translation project relied on simple, low-end digital tools, methods, and skills, yet contributed important epistemological and methodological transformations in their research process and output. This kind of transformation is precisely what constitutes digital scholarship as an essential aspect of contemporary knowledge production in the humanities, just as the low-end technical activity of Word processing brought immense transformations to humanists' work and became an integral part of "normal humanities," to paraphrase Khun.

An additional reason for differentiating between digital humanities and digital scholarship in the humanities stems from the fact that the field of digital humanities has strongholds in certain humanities disciplines, as discussed in chapter 1, while digital scholarship unfolds across the humanities. Archeology, for example, has a long history of profound engagement with technology, but does not identify with the digital humanities community. It is questionable whether humanities disciplines that have well-developed trajectories of digital scholarship would want and need to blend into the digital humanities, especially if exclusionary and prescriptive voices in this field persist.

In some of the humanities disciplines without established trajectories of digital scholarship, the entry through digital humanities has been challenging due to the field's focus on textual tools, methods, and projects. The ways of engagement with digital technologies are inevitably different across the humanities disciplines. Digital humanities, if this term remains, will thus also have to assume the plural form, standing for the *fields* of digital humanities. To that goal, relative neutrality of digital scholarship might be a better-suited route than epistemologically and methodologically overloaded track of digital humanities.

Finally, disentangling digital humanities from digital scholarship in the humanities is a prologue to rethinking a set of disciplinary, educational, organizational, and funding questions. One of the important aspects of this process is to understand how expectations formulated within the field of digital humanities might influence digital scholarship in the humanities.

Expectations

Various disciplines—sociology, economics, history and philosophy of science, and science and technology studies (STS)—have examined how expectations influence scholarly and technological change. Expectations, including repeating cycles of hype and disappointment, had an important role in shaping and establishing areas of research such as gene therapy, pharmacogenomics, nano-technology, biological computing, and so on (see Brown et al., 2003). Expectations have a multifaceted role in the early stages of a field. They help articulate visions, direct strategies, set goals, and form shared values, thus pre-disciplining the imagination about the field (see Borup et al., 2006). Scholarly innovation intrinsically focuses on the future, so expectations—or research dreams, as Kok and Wouters (2013) dub them—play a significant role by offering "elaborate discursive sketch[es] of the future state of the field" (ibid., p. 221).

Initiatives in the field of digital humanities have been part of such elaborate envisioning of digital knowledge production in the humanities. These initiatives were vital for developing digital research infrastructure in the humanities, including tools, methods, corpora, journals, professional associations, centers, and educational initiatives. This field also promoted a set of innovative principles related to digital scholarship, such as open access, interdisciplinary collaboration, and alternative career paths. Finally, these efforts facilitated more active engagement of various humanities stakeholders, from researchers to funders, fostering intellectual and financial investments in digital knowledge production in the humanities. Equally important is the role of this field in present-day humanities scholarship. Among its many accomplishments are cutting-edge research projects, continuous development of digital methods, an ever-increasing number of digital resources, a growing number of practitioners, and the ongoing education of future scholars through both informal programs and a growing number of degree-granting programs in digital humanities.

Yet, less favorable effects of this field on humanities digital knowledge production should also be assessed. One risk is that research dreams formulated within the field of digital humanities monopolize a broader, long-term transition of humanities disciplines toward digital scholarship. Despite the discourse of broad tents and developmental phases such as "digital humanities I and II" (see Davidson, 2008; Ramsay, 2013), the digital humanities community continues to promote a specific vision and version of humanities engagement with technology exemplified in recognition of core competencies, key skills, traditional values, and so on. The usefulness of these capacities for the field of digital humanities is not the subject of this analysis. The point here is that competencies, skills, and values formulated within this field cannot be promoted as the obligatory yardstick of progress and success concerning digital knowledge production in the humanities. In the transition toward digital scholarship, humanities disciplines need to develop their own research dreams, as well as their own criteria for evaluating progress toward that future, rather than passively accept externally formulated visions and standards. The diversity of scholarly practices, needs, values, and engagements with technology needs to be stimulated and rewarded in the humanities. Otherwise, the perils of prescriptive "good scholarship" might take hold, hindering alternative visions and practices on the one hand, and perpetuating cycles of expectations and disappointments on the other.

Expectations generated in the early visions of a field, which Mokyr (1991) aptly terms "hopeful monstrosities," commonly fail to meet their promises, so much so that "disappointment seems to be almost built into the way expectations operate" (Brown et al., 2003). Such built-in disappointments do not occur because people making them are unaware that those promises will be difficult, if at all possible to meet. Instead, the promises are intentionally set high as strategic resources (see Geels and Smith, 2000). Similar dynamics of tactical discursive maneuvering can be found in the field of digital humanities, starting with the strategic selection of its name, and extending to various initiatives founded and funded on the promise of advancing humanities scholarship. As previously mentioned, the Mission statement of the 4Humanities advocacy group claims that the digital humanities community has a "special potential and responsibility" in humanities scholarship, given that digital humanities "catch the eye of administrators and funding agencies who otherwise dismiss the humanities as yesterday's news." The promised potential of digital humanities is such that this field should "completely change what it means to be a humanities scholar" (Parry, 2010), and if digital humanists do not "burn away the dead wood" in humanities scholarship, humanists "will suffocate under the noxious rot of [their] own decay" (Bogost, 2010, para.10).

What promissory accounts like these do not mention is the astounding rate of unfinished and abandoned digital humanities projects (see Gibbs, 2011). Raley (2014) posits that the field of digital humanities is "particularly well positioned to exploit the expectation that we should be affectively awed by instrumentation ('oh my god, this lab, this application, is so cool,')" yet emphasizes that its "archives, centers, and labs are a veritable graveyard of discarded tools and projects" (pp. 5, 8).

Although such disappointments seem to be a predictable part in the game of expectations, they come at a price, namely damage to the credibility of various stakeholders and misallocated resources and investments. Additional problem is that expectations often put forward simplified approaches and assessments of practice, under the assumption that the overall, future-oriented vision is more significant than the presumably transient details. As a consequence, early initiatives are often technologically focused and deterministic, failing to acknowledge a complex web of cultural, economic, organizational, and other aspects shaping a socio-technical system. Kainz (2010) estimates that in the development of earlier digital humanities projects two-thirds of the time was spent "on developing the technology rather than focusing on the scholarship" (para. 3). Dombrowski (2014) similarly underlines the techno-deterministic focus on pain points that digital tools and methods can solve, without "significantly treat[ing] the possibility that humanists might focus on *needs that could not meaningfully be addressed through the development of technology*" (p. 3; italics added).

Finally, although promises and expectations do not automatically imply the proponent's liability, they do invoke reactions and counter-expectations (see Brown et al., 2003). The strong reactions that some of the promises voiced in the digital humanities provoke in other streams of humanities scholarship might be seen as a result of that dynamics. When loudly voiced yet unmet promises stand without consequence, and, moreover, become justifications for further actions, counterreactions are inevitable. For instance, funders in the digital humanities field might accept that a project fails "as long as it fails successfully," as one of my interviewees put it, namely, insomuch as it serves as a learning experience for some future projects. However, humanities scholars have a legitimate right to question such funding decisions, which feed the promise-failure loop, especially in the situation of drastic budget cuts in the humanities. Also, some of the digital humanities projects might try to shield themselves from responsibility of unmet promises by claiming the emerging character of the field. In reality, the field of digital humanities has been active long enough that its failures can be identified along with its successes. Kok and Wouters (2013) illustrate this dynamics in the area of social history, where digital humanities initiatives have been fluctuating through cycles of promises and disappointments for decades.

The need to regulate the promise/disappointment dynamics mandates developing and implementing quality control criteria for digital knowledge production in the humanities. As discussed in chapters 3 and 4, the respondents in my study unanimously noted that digital humanities as a field and as a set of practices critically lack evaluation criteria. Such a deficiency of standardization makes it a challenge for scholars, administrators, funders, and other stakeholders to responsibly answer key questions and make meaningful decisions. Having strong, accepted evaluation criteria would better prepare these decision makers to act in the face of various expectations and risks surrounding digital scholarship in the humanities. It is also important that those benchmarks combine the innovative aspects of digital scholarship with the imperatives of epistemological and methodological rigor, as well as intellectual contribution (see Cohen and Troyano, 2012).

Furthermore, as Bijker et al. (2012) point out, "Technology is a slippery term, and concepts such as 'technological change' and 'technological development' often carry a heavy interpretative load" (xii). Quality control focused on digital humanities and digital scholarship in the humanities should not draw on normative premises of "epistemic purity" or "correct knowledge" to which knowledge production in digital humanities should conform. Neither should it focus on assessing the probability of certain technological predictions concerning digital scholarship. However, developing an analytical evaluative perspective that focuses on the quality of the scholarly process and outcomes is possible and necessary. Research dreams should not be prevented or sanctioned. Yet, it is essential to encourage a widespread dialog among stakeholders to mitigate potential mistakes and resource misallocations without hindering innovation in scholarly work. As Brown and colleagues suggest, the quality control focused on robustness and pertinence of innovation should start by developing strategies for "how much inflation can be tolerated and is prudent" (2003, p. 8). Without such strategies and mechanisms of quality control, the promise and disappointment cycles will linger. Failures around unused/unusable tools and resources will continue along with rationales of a still-developing field and other revisionist theories that "tend to forget or silence complexity and contingency, transforming a resultant technology into a hero of its own making" (Borup et al., 2006: 290).

Inscribed Expectations

Scholarly expectations and visions do not only take the discursive form, but also materialize as tools, actions, and projects. Formulated as future-oriented constructs, they actually unfold in practice. Expectations about the future state of the field, as well as envisioned attributes of its practitioners, get inscribed into socio-technical systems (see Borup et al., 2006). Thus, research dreams and expectations considerably influence the scholarly discussions of technological change and their implantation in practice, as well as far-reaching implications for how scholarly fields evolve. As Brown et al. (2003) point out, these visions create a perception of inevitability, "the production of a particular narrative order that polices the future behaviour of a whole range of actors" (p. 5).

Visions and values articulated in the field of digital humanities have become inscribed in disciplinary structures such as digital humanities centers, job descriptions, university curricula, award systems, and research tools and methods. This was important for the development and strengthening of digital knowledge production in the humanities. Yet, it is equally important that understanding of humanists' engagement with technology articulated in the digital humanists does not become passively accepted as the dominant vision in the humanities. We should be aware that digital humanities has been steering the development of digital scholarship in the humanities, and to critically assess the benefits and downsides of that influence. Both discursive formulations and their embodiment in the socio-technical system need to be part of a comprehensive debate in the humanities, reflecting multiplicity of practices and perspectives. To avoid the views of a group of stakeholders from developing into presumed norms governing how all humanists engage with digital scholarship, it is essential to involve a wide range of actors, views, and visions in the deliberations of digital knowledge production in the humanities.

Different stakeholders approach, assess, and trust expectations differently, depending on their role in a given socio-technical system. If those stakeholders do not have equal voice in formulating research dreams and narratives, if they are excluded or marginalized in scholarly discussions and decisions concerning technological change, they will ultimately distrust those changes. The risk of such a development exists in the humanities. As discussed in the previous chapters, humanists overwhelmingly feel that they have no influence over the development of tools, university policies, organizational decisions, and other important elements concerning digital scholarship in the humanities. Other professionals, such as librarians, academic software developers, or managers of digital humanities centers also shared the feeling that they were too often on the recipient rather than the participant side of the decision-making processes influencing their work. A widespread dialog among the stakeholders thus needs to be embedded into all the phases—from planning to evaluation—of educational, research, and organizational initiatives concerning digital scholarship in the humanities.

Without a widespread dialog, the group of actors formulating expectations on behalf of the entire community grows overconfident about their positions and actions, neither of which are necessarily grounded in practice. As Borup et al. (2006) point out, "a heightened sense of confidence often reflects a detachment or distance from the acute uncertainties more usually experienced by researchers at the 'coal face' of conducting the research on which a future field will depend" (p. 292). In digital humanities, this kind of detachment can be found among the administrators or theorists reliant on the so-called "I-methodology" (see Akrich 1995), which promotes authors' views or preferences as representative of the humanities scholarship. It is thus important to pay attention to recommendations coming from digital humanities centers, whose work on the ground reflects practices, difficulties, and needs of the wider humanities community. The transition of humanities disciplines toward digital scholarship is a complex process that needs to be handled in an equally complex, systematic, and inclusive manner. This necessitates a continuous dialog among all stakeholders to ensure an organizational framework that supports scholar innovation, yet avoids restrictive top-down initiatives formulated irrespective of practice and with little or no support for alternative and spontaneous developments.

Providing support for alternative developments is another significant function of expectations, which often help establish intellectual and physical spaces where experimentation and innovation are encouraged and sheltered. Digital humanities initiatives and centers provide such protected spaces for exploring innovative uses of digital technologies in the humanities. Yet, as Kok and Wouters warn (2013), insulating digital scholarship in such specialized spaces can also be disengaging with regard to other humanities activities. It is therefore needed to position digital scholarship both conceptually and physically intertwined with other streams of humanities scholarship. Prevailing organizational strategy, however, often places digital scholarship in libraries and other spaces outside the central disciplinary workflows. This tendency seems as being built around Liu's (2009) metaphor of digital technologies as carriers of viruses that "transmit alien disciplinary genes from other paradigms of knowledge" to the humanities (p. 17). The question then arises whether digital humanities centers and similar specialized units shelter innovative humanities work from potentially dogmatic approaches in the "normal humanities" or keep the latter immune from "dangerous epistemic virus." As previously stated, confining digital scholarship to digital humanities centers is potentially damaging in the long run because those centers might become spaces that isolate rather than connect digital scholarship to the humanities.

Digital scholarship is a far-reaching and long-lasting development, and the entire humanities' socio-technical system will need to codevelop with these transformations. The approach to these transformations needs to be much more comprehensive than reshuffling space and employees into new units, as so often happens at universities today. Universities need to promote hybridity of research, workforce, and knowledge production in the overall university system rather than provide isolated playgrounds for silo-style work.

Specialized units, such as digital humanities centers, should not remain the main locus of digital scholarship in the humanities. The organizational and financial structure of these centers is not robust enough to support the transition of humanities disciplines toward digital scholarship. Instead, digital scholarship in the humanities needs to be part of humanities departments and wider university initiatives. Liu (2009) correctly states that "digital humanities will ultimately matter, or not at all, *inside* the department," pointing out that departments remain the primary locations of humanists' research and teaching engagements (p. 21; italics in the original). He argues that physical location and organizational structure of an activity significantly shape its intellectual attributes and effects; hence, "in-house" digital knowledge production enables humanists to develop greater familiarity and influence over this stream of scholarship.

In addition to research, educational activities in digital scholarship also need to be part of humanities departments and intradepartmental initiatives. This applies to both student and faculty education. As long as humanists' interaction with digital tools, methods, and resources is treated merely as a technical skill that can be taught by nonexpert personnel (or robots) (Amato 2014), it will be difficult to achieve substantial scholarly results and excite academics about digital scholarship. Raley (2014) rightly points out that "academic service staff providing skills-based training [...] and performing service work for 'clueless arts and humanities scholars,' can tell us something about both the field and the university" (p. 7). Instead of skilled-based training, humanities education in digital scholarship needs a comprehensive framework encompassing epistemological, methodological, technical, and sociocultural aspects of digital knowledge production. These include developing understanding of digital and other types of data, fostering critical reflection on digital objects of inquiry, comprehending the influence of algorithmic processes on humanities investigations, and so on. Similarly, digital methods training should include systematic deliberation on methodological decisions influencing research process and results, epistemological and ethical challenges of digital scholarship, making choice of digital tools and methods as best suited for specific research questions, and so forth.

This approach is important for both student and faculty education. In the same way student education in digital scholarship is increasingly organized within dedicated humanities programs and departments, the same should be the case with respect to senior academics. The results of my study reveal that humanists favor and best learn in practice, when instruction is closely related to their area of study and when it unfolds organically through collaboration and discussion with peers or graduate students (see chapter 4). My respondents pointed at higher and more successful learning uptake when attending conferences rather than university-organized workshops. At conferences, they see how their peers engage with digital tools and methods to deal with research challenges similar to their own, thus gaining perspective on the potentials of digital scholarship for their work.[5] My study also suggests that humanists like to discuss methodological, epistemological, or technical features of digital tools in social media or via e-mail, to exchange experiences, and to learn from each other. To promote learning among senior scholars, a variety of learning methods should thus be harvested, instead of limiting training to sessions at libraries and digital humanities centers. Furthermore, these educational activities should not restrain the generative potential of digital scholarship in the humanities through the exclusive focus on research themes, methods, and skills recognized in the field of digital humanities. Humanities scholars do not necessarily need or want to be digital humanists, as currently conceived. They do, however, need and overwhelmingly want to be scholars competent at teaching and conducting research in the digital age.

University administrators and funders should support the efforts of humanities faculty to become competent digital scholars. As one of my interviewees, a program officer in a major humanities foundation points out, the goal should be "to fund training for scholars even if they don't want to be a digital humanist in the sense that they're building their own tools and their programming, but more along the lines of users of digital technology within their own research." This kind of funders' support to digital scholarship in the humanities, not necessarily to digital humanities, is crucial. While digital humanities might indeed be "a term possessed of enough currency and escape velocity...to get funds allocated," as Kirschenbaum argues (2012, p. 417), it is necessary for both university administrators and funders to listen to those humanists' voices not regularly represented in the digital humanities discourse and to support their needs concerning digital scholarship. In the same manner, it is vital that education in digital scholarship becomes administratively recognized as part of scholars' professional development included in their paid time and activity, as well as in their promotion dossiers. As long as specialization in digital scholarship remains an administratively unrecognized add-on to scholars' already over-burdened schedules, there is little chance that it will gain wide acceptance in the humanities community.

Beyond Expectations

The pervasiveness of technology in different segments of contemporary life prompts techno-deterministic visions and sentiments about the future, commonly framed as utopian/technophile or dystopian/technophobe approaches. These visions share an underlying assumption of inevitability, a sense of lack of control over the future. While it is certain that various segments of life will profoundly change through their future cocreation with technology, any presumed certainties about specific directions and/or modes of development should always be questioned. "Futures are not inevitable but rather, they are 'fought for,' resisted or embraced," Brown and colleagues (2000) remind us.

The same message—that the future needs to be fought for—applies to digital scholarship in the humanities. The fight I am suggesting does not involve perpetuating exclusionary, accusatory, or dismissing discourses and actions either concerning "digital" or "mainstream" humanities, nor the combat for resources, jobs, and authority. Instead, it should be the fight for diversity and for recognition of opposed values, practices, and expectations along the lines of Liu's universal humanism. Regardless the size of any current disciplinary "tent," digital knowledge production is intellectually, technically, and culturally unbounded. Whatever we might currently expect and fight for, the future will always be otherwise. Even a cursory look at the history of science and technology shows that forcefully advocated "truths" or "hopeful monstrosities" of one era lose their "disruptive innovativeness," "revolutionary potential," even "meaningfulness" in the face of a new era. Let us thus approach humanities knowledge production in the digital age as good ethnographers, who rejoice in the chance to always be surprised and accept the axiom that "everything could always be otherwise."

Appendix

INTERVIEW QUESTIONS FOR HUMANITIES SCHOLARS

Date and time:

Location:

Interviewer:

Interviewee:

DEMOGRAPHIC DATA

Type of Institution	University/Govt./Private Foundation/Commercial/Other
Job Title	_____
Academic Background	_____
Highest Degree	_____
Field of Study	_____
Age	___ 21–30 ___ 31–40 ___ 41–50 ___ 51–60 ___ >60
Gender	___ male ___ female
Native Language	___ Dutch ___ other _____

INTERVIEW QUESTIONS

- What do you understand by digital research tools and methods?
- What digital research tools and methods do you use in your daily work?
- What digital tools and methods do you have the most success doing research with? Why?

- How do you decide which digital tools and methods to use?
- For how long have you been using digital tools and methods in your research practice?
- How well do you feel digital tools and methods are integrated in your research practice?
- What sort of research questions do digital tools and methods help you answer? What sort of research questions are these tools and methods best suited for?
- What is the role of digital tools and methods at various stages of your research process?
- What impact of digital tools and methods on your work practices would you identify as most important?
- What impact of digital tools and methods on your research results would you identify as most important?
- What, if anything, did you learn about your field of study through the use of digital research tools and methods? What did you learn about your own research practice?
- What do you see as key challenges of using digital tools and methods in your area of research?
- What do you see as short-term benefits of using digital tools and methods in your field of research? What are the potential long-term benefits?
- In your field of study, has use of digital tools and methods created research questions that could not have been asked before?
- What research trajectories do you see developing in your research area as a result of incorporating digital tools and methods?
- Where do humanities researchers learn and where do they teach digital research methods?
- How do you evaluate the quality of digital humanities projects? Which criteria do you use?
- In your view, what kind of influence do humanities researchers have on the design and development of digital tools, methods and resources for humanities research?
- In your opinion/experience, what are special considerations to be taken into account when developing tools, methods and resources for humanities research?
- What would be an example of a digital tool feature the tool developers had not planned and foreseen?
- What, if anything, would improve your experience in using digital tools and methods?
- Is there anything I did not ask and you think would be important to say?

FIELDWORK NOTES

FIELDWORK COMMENTS

INTERVIEW QUESTIONS FOR ADMINISTRATORS OF
DIGITAL HUMANITIES CENTERS

Date and time:

Location:

Interviewer:

Interviewee:

DEMOGRAPHIC DATA

Type of Institution	University/Govt./Private Foundation/Commercial/Other
Job Title	_____
Academic Background	_____
Highest Degree	_____
Field of Study	_____
Age	____ 21–30 ____ 31–40 ____ 41–50 ____ 51–60 ____ >60
Gender	____ male ____ female
Native Language	____ Dutch ____ other _____

INTERVIEW QUESTIONS

- With which goals in mind was this center launched?

- Who were your main collaborators in setting up the center? What were the reactions among the colleagues, students, and administrators?

- What do you see as the role of your center in humanities scholarship?

- What do you see as the role of this center within the system of your university?

- In your experience, what are the main challenges of developing a digital humanities center? What special considerations should be taken into account when developing a digital humanities center?

- In what ways, if any, have your expectations related to the center and its role changed over time?

- What are the main challenges of running a digital humanities center?

- In your view, are digital humanities centers more effective when organized around a particular research area or around a research community? Why?

- How do you evaluate the quality of digital humanities projects? Which criteria do you use?

- What do you see as short-term benefits of using digital tools, methods, and resources in humanities research?

- What are the potential long-term benefits of using digital tools, methods, and resources in humanities research?

- What research trajectories do you see developing in the humanities as a result of incorporating digital tools, methods, and resources?

- What are the main challenges of incorporating digital tools, methods, and resources in humanities scholarship?

- Where do humanities researchers learn and where do they teach digital research methods?

- What do you see as key challenges of developing digital tools and resources for humanities research?

- In your view, what kind of influence do humanities scholars have on the design and development of tools, services, and resources provided in your center?

- What special considerations should be taken into account when developing digital tools and resources for humanities research?

- In your view, what is the future of digital humanities centers?

- Is there anything I did not ask and you think would be important to say?

FIELDWORK NOTES

FIELDWORK COMMENTS

INTERVIEW QUESTIONS FOR DEVELOPERS

Date and time:

Location:

Interviewer:

Interviewee:

DEMOGRAPHIC DATA

Type of Institution	University/Govt./Private Foundation/Commercial/Other
Job Title	_____
Academic Background	_____
Highest Degree	_____
Field of Study	_____
Age	____ 21–30 ____ 31–40 ____ 41–50 ____ 51–60 ____ >60
Gender	____ male ____ female
Native Language	____ Dutch ____ other _____

INTERVIEW QUESTIONS

- What do you understand by digital research tools and methods?
- What do you see as key challenges of developing digital tools and resources for humanities research?
- In your view, which features should a humanities research tool have? What makes for an effective humanities research tool?
- In your experience, what kind of influence do humanities researchers have on the design and development of digital tools and resources for humanities research?
- In your opinion/experience, what are special considerations to be taken into account when developing tools and resources for humanities research?

- What would be an example of a digital tool feature the developers had not planned and foreseen?

- What is your experience about the interaction between humanities scholars and tool developers?

- What is your vision about the interaction between humanities scholars and tool developers?

- What do you see as short-term benefits of using digital tools, methods, and resources in humanities research? What are the potential long-term benefits?

- In your view, what sort of scholarly questions are digital tools and methods best suited for?

- What do you see as the role of digital tools and methods at various stages of a research process?

- How do you evaluate the quality of humanities digital research tools and resources? Which criteria do you use?

- Is there anything I did not ask and you think would be important to say?

FIELDWORK NOTES

FIELDWORK COMMENTS

INTERVIEW QUESTIONS FOR FUNDERS

Date and time:

Location:

Interviewer:

Interviewee:

DEMOGRAPHIC DATA

Type of Institution	University/Govt./Private Foundation/Commercial/Other
Job Title	_____
Academic Background	_____
Highest Degree	_____
Field of Study	_____
Age	____ 21–30 ____ 31–40 ____ 41–50 ____ 51–60 ____ >60
Gender	____ male ____ female
Native Language	____ Dutch ____ other _____

INTERVIEW QUESTIONS

- Could you, please, tell me about the main goals of your organization?

- In what ways does your organization define areas of funding?

- What distinguishes the approach of your organization to the projects you are funding?

- What are the priority areas of your organization in terms of supporting digital research in the humanities?

- What are your main requirements for project applications in the area of digital humanities?

- How do you evaluate the quality of project applications in the area of digital humanities? Which criteria do you use?

- How do you evaluate the impact of the projects you funded in the area of digital humanities?

- What is the usual life cycle of the projects you fund?

- What is your approach to funding educational activities focused on digital scholarship in the humanities?

- What is your approach to data sharing, open access, and open license concerning the content and tools developed within the projects you fund?

- What do you see as the main short-term benefits of using digital technologies in the humanities? What are the potential long-term benefits?

- What do you see as the main challenges in digital humanities?

- What research trajectories do you see developing in the humanities as a result of incorporating digital tools, methods, and resources?

- In your view, what kind of influence do humanities researchers have on the design and development of digital tools and resources for humanities research?

- What do you see as key challenges of developing digital tools and resources for humanities research?

- In your view, what is the future of digital scholarship in the humanities?

- Is there anything I did not ask and you think would be important to say?

FIELDWORK NOTES

FIELDWORK COMMENTS

INTERVIEW QUESTIONS

Date and time:

Location:

Interviewer:

Interviewee:

DEMOGRAPHIC DATA

Age

• 21–30   • 31–40v   • 41–50   • 51–60   • >60

Gender

I identify my gender as _____ (fill in the blank)

Current academic position

• Tenure-track faculty
• Tenured faculty
• Fixed-term faculty
• Instructor
• Graduate student
• Other (please specify)

Primary area(s) of research:

INTERVIEW QUESTIONS

- What do you understand by digital research tools and methods?
- Which digital tools and methods do you use in your daily work?
- Could you, please, guide me though this diagram [Figure 2.1: *Research Workflow*, p. 28] and tell me which digital tools and methods you use in each of the research phases?
- What digital tools and methods do you have the most success doing research with? Why?
- How do you decide which digital tools and methods to use?

- For how long have you been using digital tools in your research practice?

- What is the role of digital tools and methods at various stages of your research process?

- What impact of digital tools and methods on your work practices would you identify as most important?

- What impact of digital tools and methods on your research results would you identify as most important?

- What have you experienced as key challenges of using digital tools and methods in your research?

- What do you see as key challenges of using digital tools and methods in your area of research?

- What do you see as short-term benefits of using digital tools and methods in your field of research? What are the potential long-term benefits?

- What research trajectories do you see developing in your research area as a result of incorporating digital tools and methods?

- Where do researchers in your field of study learn and teach digital research methods?

- What is the role of librarians and the library in facilitating your research process?

- How confident do you feel in your data management skills? What do you think could improve those skills?

- What do you see as your most lasting scholarly output? What strategies do you use to curate and/or preserve that output?

- Who should ensure longer-term access to your work?

- Where would you want your personal scholarly archive to reside? Who should have access to it?

- In your view, what kind of influence do researchers have on the design and development of digital research tools?

- What kind of influence do researchers have on the development of new library search tools and library resources (collections and more)?

- In your opinion/experience, what are special considerations to be taken into account when developing digital research tools and resources?

- What, if anything, would improve your experience in using digital tools, methods, and resources?

- Is there anything I did not ask and you think would be important to say?

FIELDWORK NOTES

FIELDWORK COMMENTS

Online Survey Questions

1. What is your age?

   - 17–21
   - 21–30
   - 31–40
   - 41–50
   - 51–60
   - >60

2. What is your gender?

   - Female
   - Male
   - No answer

3. What is your current academic standing?

   - Tenure-track faculty member
   - Tenured faculty member
   - Fixed-term faculty member
   - Instructor
   - Graduate student
   - Undergraduate student
   - Other (please explain)

4. What is your academic college?

   - College of Agricultural Sciences
   - College of Arts and Architecture
   - College of Business
   - College of Communications
   - College of Earth and Mineral Sciences
   - College of Education
   - College of Engineering
   - College of Health and Human Development
   - College of Information Sciences and Technology
   - School of International Affairs
   - School of Law
   - College of the Liberal Arts
   - College of Medicine
   - School of Nursing
   - College of Science
   - Graduate School
   - Honors College
   - University Libraries Other (please specify)

5. Where do you most frequently search for new articles, books, or other information relevant to your research and/or work? (Check all that apply)

- The library catalog
- Library databases (ProQuest, MUSE, ERIC, Web of Science, ScienceDirect, etc.)
- Google
- Google Scholar
- Other Internet search engine (Bing, Yahoo!, etc.)
- Other

6. Are you storing (on a computer or online) materials relevant to your research and work?

- Yes
- No

7. What kinds of research materials are you storing? (select all that apply)

- Word documents
- Data files and/or sets
- Images
- PDF documents
- Web pages
- Spreadsheets
- Email messages
- Email attachments
- Presentation files
- Other

8. Where are you storing information and materials? (select all that apply)

- Computer hard drive (i.e., My documents folder, other computer folders)
- Dropbox
- Google Drive / Google Docs
- Other Cloud-based Storage Service
- Evernote
- PDF management software (such as Papers or ReadCube)
- Citation Management software (such as *Endnote*, *Mendeley*, or *Zotero*)
- Other

9. Do you use citation management software (*Endnote*, *Mendeley*, *Refworks*, *Zotero*, etc.) to create bibliographies and/or organize references?

- Yes
- No

9a. You indicated that you use citation management software. Which software program/service do you use?

- *Endnote*
- *Mendeley*
- *Zotero*
- *Refworks*
- *Sente*
- *ReadCube*
- Papers
- Other

10. Do you use any software / online services for sharing your research materials/ data with others?

- Yes
- No

10a. You indicated that you share materials/information with others. Please indicate which program(s) / service(s) you use:

- Dropbox
- Citation Management software (*Endnote, Mendeley, Zotero*, etc.)
- Evernote
- Google Drive / Google Docs
- Shared folder on local computer network
- Emailing files to others
- PDF management software (such as Papers or ReadCube)
- Other Cloud-based sharing / storage service
- Other

11. Do you make back-up or additional copies of important materials?

- Yes
- No

11a. You indicated that you make back-up or additional copies of important materials. Please tell us how you do this:

- Print out and store copies of important documents
- On my computer
- On a cloud server (Dropbox, Google Drive, etc.)
- On an external hard drive
- On my U drive
- On a flash drive
- On a CD

- On a personal or department server
- In my PASS space
- On an ITS server
- Other

12. How often do you back-up your computer files?

- Daily
- Weekly
- Monthly
- Never
- Continually (I use a site that automatically backs up materials, such as Dropbox or Google Drive)
- Other

13. Do you regularly destroy or remove files that are no longer useful or necessary to you?

- Yes
- No

14. It is easy for me to find the research articles and other information I need for my research.

- Strongly agree
- Agree
- Neutral
- Disagree
- Strongly disagree

15. It is easy for me to store the research articles and other information I need for my research.

- Strongly agree
- Agree
- Neutral
- Disagree
- Strongly disagree

16. It is easy for me to cite the research articles and other information I need for my research.

- Strongly agree
- Agree
- Neutral
- Disagree
- Strongly disagree

17. It is easy for me to save/archive the research materials and data I need for my research.

    - Strongly agree
    - Agree
    - Neutral
    - Disagree
    - Strongly disagree

18. It is easy for me to share with others the research materials and data I use/need for my research.

    - Strongly agree
    - Agree
    - Neutral
    - Disagree
    - Strongly disagree

19. I have lost computer files or other information important to me.

    - Yes
    - No

20. There are files that I would like to currently use that I can no longer access (because they are lost, obsolete, in an older format):

    - Yes
    - No

21. If you indicated that there are files you would like to currently use that you can no longer access, please tell us why:

    - File(s) were lost
    - Files are in an obsolete format (i.e., 3.5 inch floppy, zip disk, etc.)
    - Files were left behind on an old computer
    - Files were accidentally deleted
    - Other (please indicate what)

22. What kinds of training programs do you feel the library at your university should offer?

    - Research help (library database, Google Scholar)
    - Web applications for organizing research (e.g., RSS feeds, blogs, wikis, social bookmarking
    - Citation Management (e.g., *EndNote*, *RefWorks*, *Zotero*)
    - Personal archiving/digital preservation assistance
    - Management of research assets/data
    - University repository service
    - Other

Notes

Introduction

1. For the history of this term, please see chapter 1.
2. The project name draws on "alfa" as a designator for the humanities (compared with gamma for the social sciences and beta for the natural sciences), hence Alfalab translates as Humanities lab.
3. *Digitizing Words of Power* was an initiative associated with the project *The Power of Words*, organized and led by Dr. Jacqueline Borsje, a researcher at the University of Amsterdam. I was part of this initiative together with my *Alfalab* colleague, Anne Beaulieu, as well as with our KNAW colleagues from the Meertens Institute.
4. See http://www.oii.ox.ac.uk/research/projects/?id=58.
5. See http://scholarlyworkflow.org/publications/.
6. *InterfaceLab* research group was part of the Virtual Knowledge Studio for the Humanities and Social Sciences (VKS) of the KNAW, and it included three VKS researchers—Anne Beaulieu, Charles van den Heuvel, and myself. Later on, InterfaceLab became part of the eHumanities initiative of the KNAW (see http://www.ehumanities.nl/).

1 Digital Humanities as Theory and Practice

1. As S. Hockey ("The History of Humanities Computing," in *A Companion to Digital Humanities*, ed. Susan Schreibman, Ray Siemens, John Unsworth [Oxford: Blackwell, 2004]) observes, "The main application of personal computers was that shared with all other disciplines, namely word processing" (para. 30).
2. For methodological uncertainties among collections, editions, archives, and databases, see Price (2009), http://www.digitalhumanities.org/dhq/vol/3/3/000053/000053.html.
3. The ADHO "About" section lists a series of similar designator changes. For instance, the European Association for Digital Humanities was founded in 1978 as the Association for Literary and Linguistic Computing, while Canadian Society for Digital Humanities was founded in 1986 as the Consortium for Computers in the Humanities (see http://adho.org/about).

4. In 2008, this unit was renamed the Office of Digital Humanities.
5. See http://dsh.oxfordjournals.org/long_live_the_journal.

2 Workflows of Digital Scholars

* This chapter is partially based on the article by Smiljana Antonijević and Ellysa Stern Cahoy, "Personal Library Curation: An Ethnographic Study of Scholars' Information Practices," *portal: Libraries and the Academy* 14.2 (2014): 287–306.

1. This model was inspired by similar diagrams; see DCC Curation Lifecycle Model (http://www.dcc.ac.uk/resources/curation-lifecycle-model) and Data Life Cycle (http://libraries.mit.edu/guides/subjects/data-management/cycle.html).
2. The conceptualization of a digital tool was left open to respondents' interpretation and definition.
3. The respondents in this study broadly define discovery search as "finding things you don't know exist."
4. Instead of trying to mirror users' Google experience, some academic libraries have opted for different solutions. For instance, Utrecht University Library in the Netherlands has recently completed a study among its users, and, after finding the prevailing use of commercial services for information search, decided to close down its own local discovery tool (see Kortekaas, S., [2012], "Thinking the Unthinkable: A Library Without a Catalogue— Reconsidering the Future of Discovery Tools for Utrecht University Library," Association of European Research Libraries, http://www.libereurope.eu/blog/thinking-the-unthinkable-alibrary-without-a-catalogue-reconsidering-the-future-of-discovery-tools [accessed July 28, 2014]).
5. In this study, storing refers to handling research materials in current use in ways that enable fast access and recovery of those materials.
6. Concerning the activities of storing and organizing research materials we see again that academics, when having an option to select, largely opt for commercial tools, as it was the case with electronic search and access services.
7. In this study, archiving is understood as handling of research materials that are no longer in use, but scholars need or want to preserve them over longer periods of time.
8. See http://www.ncbi.nlm.nih.gov/genbank/.

3 Disciplinary (Re)Orientations

1. See https://books.google.com/ngrams.
2. See http://digitalhumanities.org/answers/.
3. See http://dirt.projectbamboo.org/).
4. See https://digitalresearchtools.pbworks.com/w/page/17801672/FrontPage.

4 Organizational Patterns

1. "We felt very strongly that we wanted humanists to collaborate, more or less along the lines of a science model, so for us it was not just about digital humanities, but collaboration," said the vice director of this center.
2. See chapter 2.
3. Some of the questions that my interviewees at digital humanities centers routinely deliberate include: "At what point do we step in to interject and posit something that is interesting to everybody? How hard do we push on that? Do we just let these people continue their conversations?"
4. The field of digital humanities is often described as a "hybrid domain" (see http://www.digitalhumanities.org/dhq/vol/001/1/000007/000007.html), hence designators such as hybrid pedagogy, hybrid research, hybrid scholars, and so on.

5 Beyond Expectations

1. See http://www.projectbamboo.org/.
2. See Kirschenbaum, 2009.
3. See chapter 2.
4. See chapter 1.
5. These organic ways of learning are not associated only with humanities scholars. My interviews with academic tool developers and technical support staff showed that they also learn through shadowing senior colleagues and by attending professional conferences.

References

Akrich, M. (1995). "User Representations: Practices, Methods and Sociology." In *Managing Technology in Society: The Approach of Constructive Technology Assessment*, edited by Rip, A., Misa, T. J., and Schot, J. London: Pinter Publishers, 167–184.

Alvarado, R. (2011). *The Digital Humanities Situation.* Available at http://transducer.ontoligent.com/?p=717, accessed July 16, 2014.

Amato, A. M. (2014). "Bioinc Buddies: Robots Nancy and Vincent Make History at Westport Library." *Westport News*, October 4, 2014. Available at http://www.westport-news.com/news/article/Bionic-buddies-Robots-Nancy-and-Vincent-make-5798482.php.

Anderson, J. Q., and Rainie, L. (2012). "Millennials Will Benefit and Suffer Due to Their Hyperconnected Lives." *Pew Research Center's Internet& American Life Project.* Available at http://www.pewinternet.org/files/old-media//Files/Reports/2012/PIP_Future_of_Internet_2012_Young_brains_PDF.pdf, accessed August 8, 2014.

Antonijević, S., Dormans, S., and Wyatt, S. (2013). "Working in Virtual Knowledge: Affective Labor in Scholarly Communication". In *Virtual Knowledge*, edited by Wouters, P., Beaulieu, A., Scharnhorst, A., and Wyatt, S. Cambridge, MA: MIT Press, 57–89.

Asher, A. D., Duke, M. L., and Wilson, S. (2013). "Paths of Discovery: Comparing the Search Effectiveness of EBSCO Discovery Service, Summon, Google Scholar, and Conventional Library Resources." College and Research Libraries, 464–488. Available at http://crl.acrl.org/content/74/5/464.full.pdf, accessed September 15, 2014.

Asher, A., Deards, K., Esteva, M., Halbert, M., Jahnke, L., Jordan, C., Keralis, S. D. C., Kulasekaran, S., Moen, W. E., Stark, S., Urban, T., and Walling, D. (2013). *Research Data Management: Principles, Practices, and Prospects.* Washington, DC: Council on Library and Information Resources.

Barth, F. (1995). "Other Knowledge and Other Ways of Knowing." *Journal of Anthropological Research* 51.1: 65–68.

Beaulieu, A. (2004). "From Brainbank to Database: The Informational Turn in the Study of the Brain." *Studies in History and Philosophy of Biological and Biomedical Sciences* 35: 367–390.

Berry, D. M. (ed.). (2012). *Understanding Digital Humanities*. Basingstoke, UK: Palgrave Macmillan.

Bijker, W. E., Hughes, T. P., and Pinch, T. (2012/1987). *The Social Construction of Technological Systems: New Directions in the Sociology and History of Technology*. Cambridge, MA: MIT Press.

Bijker, W. E., and Law, J. (1992). *Shaping Technology / Building Society: Studies in Sociotechnical Change*. Cambridge, MA: MIT Press

Bogost, I. (2010). *The Turtlenecked Hairshirt: Fetid and Fragrant Futures for the Humanities*. Available at http://bogost.com/writing/blog/the_turtlenecked_hairshirt/, accessed September 19, 2014.

Borup, M., Brown, N., Konrad, K., and Van Lente, H. (2006). "The Sociology of Expectations in Science and Technology." *Technology Analysis & Strategic Management* 18.3/4: 285–298.

Bourdieu, P. (1988). *Homo Academicus*. Palo Alto, CA: Stanford University Press.

Bowker, G. (2000). "Biodiversity Datadiversity." *Social Studies of Science* 30.5: 643–684.

Bowker, G., and Star, S. (1999). *Sorting Things Out: Classification and Its Consequences*. Cambridge, MA: MIT Press.

Brabazon, T. (2007). *The University of Google*. Hampshire, UK: Ashgate.

Brey, P. (2005). "The Epistemology and Ontology of Human-Computer Interaction." *Minds and Machines* 15: 383–398.

Brown, S., Ross, R., Gerrard, D., Grass, M., and Bryson, S. (2006). The RePAH Project. Available at http://repah.dmu.ac.uk/report/pdfs/RePAHReport-Complete.pdf, accessed October 7, 2014.

Brown, N., Rip, A., and Van Lente, H. (2003). *Expectations In & About Science and Technology*. A Background Paper for the "Expectations" Workshop of June 13–14, 2003. Available at http://www.york.ac.uk/satsu/expectations/Utrecht%202003/Background%20paper%20version%2014May03.pdf, accessed October 5, 2014

Bulger, M. E., Meyer, E. T., De la Flor, G., Terras, M., Wyatt, S., Jirotka, M., Eccles, K., and McCarthy Madsen, C. (2011). *Reinventing Research? Information Practices in the Humanities*. A Research Information Network Report. Available at http://ssrn.com/abstract=1859267 or http://dx.doi.org/10.2139/ssrn.1859267, accessed August 5, 2014.

Burdick, A., Drucker, J., Lunenfeld, P., Presner, T., and Schnapp. J. (2012). *Digital_Humanities*. Cambridge, MA: MIT Press.

Bush, W. (1945). "As We May Think." *The Atlantic*. Available at http://www.theatlantic.com/magazine/archive/1945/07/as-we-may-think/303881/, accessed September 8, 2014.

Carlile, P. R. (2002). "A Pragmatic View of Knowledge and Boundaries: Boundary Objects in New Product Development." *Organization Science* 13.4: 442–455.

Chun, W. H. K., and Rhody, L. M. (2014). "Working the Digital Humanities: Uncovering Shadows between the Dark and the Light." *Differences* 25.1: 1–25.

Clark, T. (1985). *A Handbook of Computational Chemistry: A Practical Guide to Chemical Structure and Energy Calculations*. New York: Wiley.

Cohen, D. J., and Troyano, J. F. (2012). "Closing the Evaluation Gap." *Journal of Digital Humanities* 1.4. Available at http://journalofdigitalhumanities.org/1-4/closing-the-evaluation-gap/, accessed December 8, 2014.

Craig, R. T. (1999). "Communication Theory as a Field." *Communication Theory*, 9.2: 119–161.

Cramer, C. J. (2013). *Essentials of Computational Chemistry: Theories and Models.* Chichester, West Sussex: John Wiley & Sons.

Davidson, C. (2012). "Humanities 2.0: Promise, Perils, Predictions." In *Debates in the Digital Humanities*, edited by Gold, M. K. Minneapolis, MN: University of Minnesota Press, 476–489.

Deegan, M., and Tanner, S. (2002). *Digital Futures: Strategies for the Information Age.* London: Library Association.

Denzin, N., and Giardina, M. D. (2008). *Qualitative Inquiry and the Politics of Evidence.* Walnut Creek, CA: Left Coast Press.

Digital Humanities Manifesto 2.0. (2009). Available at http://manifesto.humanities.ucla.edu/2009/05/29/the-digital-humanities-manifesto-20/, accessed October 7, 2014.

Dombrowksi, Q. (2014). "What Ever Happened to Project Bamboo." *Literary and Linguistic Computing* 29.3: 326–339. Available at https://rd-alliance.org/system/files/filedepot/136/Lit%20Linguist%20Computing-2014-Dombrowski-llc-fqu026.pdf, accessed December 6, 2014.

Drucker, J. (2009). *SpecLab: Digital Aesthetics and Projects in Speculative Computing.* Chicago, IL: University of Chicago Press.

Drucker, J. (2012). "Humanistic Theory and Digital Scholarship." In *Debates in the Digital Humanities*, edited by Gold, M. K. Minneapolis: University of Minnesota Press, 85–95.

Dunn, S. (2014). "Digital Humanists: If You Want Tenure, Do Double the Work." The Chronicle of Higher Education Vitae, January 5, 2014. Available at https://chroniclevitae.com/news/249-digital-humanists-if-you-want-tenure-do-double-the-work#sthash.1aKf7QCx.dpuf, accessed August 8, 2014.

Forsythe, D. E. (2001). *Studying Those Who Study Us: An Anthropologist in the World of Artificial Intelligence.* Stanford, CA: Stanford University Press.

Fraser, M., and Puwar, N. (2008). "Introduction: Intimacy in Research." *History of the Human Sciences* 21.4: 1–16.

Fraistat, N. (2012). "The Function of Digital Humanities Centers at the Present Time." In *Debates in the Digital Humanities*, edited by Gold, M. K. Minneapolis: University of Minnesota Press, 181–191.

Fiormonte, D. (2012). "Towards a Cultural Critique of the Digital Humanities." *Historical Social Research* 37.141: 59–76.

Fitzpatrick, K. (2012). "The Humanities, Done Digitally." In *Debates in the Digital Humanities*, edited by Gold, M. K. Minneapolis: University of Minnesota Press, 12–15.

Galison, P. L. (1997). *Image and Logic: A Material Culture of Microphysics.* Chicago. IL: University of Chicago Press.

Garfield, E. (1955). "Citation Indexes for Science: A New Dimension in Documentation through Association of Ideas." *Science* 122: 108–111.

Geels, F., and Smit, W. (2000). "Failed Technology Futures: Pitfalls and Lessons from a Historical Survey." *Futures* 32.9–10: 867–885.

Geertz, C. (1973). *The Interpretation of Cultures*. New York: Basic Books.

Gibs, F. W., and Owens, T. J. (2012). "The Hermeneutics of Data and Historical Writing." In *Writing History in the Digital Age*, edited by Jack Dougherty and Kristen Nawrotzki. University of Michigan Press, Trinity College web-book edition. Available at http://writinghistory.trincoll.edu/data/gibbs-owens-2012-spring/, accessed October 10, 2014.

Gill, R. (2010), "Breaking the Silence: The Hidden Injuries of the Neoliberal University." In *Secrecy and Silence in the Research Process: Feminist Reflections*, edited by Róisín Ryan-Flood and Rosalind Gill. London: Routledge, 228–244.

Gold, M. K. (ed.). (2012). *Debates in the Digital Humanities*. Minneapolis: University of Minnesota Press.

Gross, A. G. (1990). *The Rhetoric of Science*. Cambridge, MA: Harvard University Press.

Gusfield, D. (1997). *Algorithms on Strings, Trees and Sequences: Computer Science and Computational Biology*. Cambridge, UK: Cambridge University Press.

Hagen, J. B. (2001). "The Introduction of Computers into Systematic Research in the United States during the 1960s." *Studies in History and Philosophy of Biological and Biomedical Sciences* 32.2: 291–314.

Hayles, N. K. (2012). "How We Think: Transforming Power and Digital Technologies." In *Understanding Digital Humanities*, edited by Berry, D. M. Basingstoke, UK: Palgrave Macmillan, 42–66.

Hine, C. (2006). *New Infrastructures for Knowledge Production: Understanding E-science*. Hershey, PA: IGI Global.

Hine, C. (2008). *Systematics as Cyberscience: Computers, Change and Continuity in Science*. Cambridge, MA: MIT Press.

Hockey, S. (2004). "The History of Humanities Computing." In *A Companion to Digital Humanities*, edited by Susan Schreibman, Ray Siemens, John Unsworth. Oxford: Blackwell. Available at http://www.digitalhumanities.org/companion/view?docId=blackwell/9781405103213/9781405103213.xml&chunk.id=ss1-2-1, accessed July 16, 2014.

Huggett, J. (2012). "Core or Periphery? Digital Humanities from an Archaeological Perspective." *Historical Social Research* 37.3: 86–105. Available at http://nbn-resolving.de/urn:nbn:de:0168-ssoar-378333, accessed July 16, 2014.

Ingold, T. (2002/1994). *Companion Encyclopedia of Anthropology*. New York: Routledge

Jankowski, N. (2009). *e-Research: Transformation in Scholarly Practice*. New York: Routledge.

Jasanoff, S. (2004). "Ordering Knowledge, Ordering Society." In *States of Knowledge: The Co-production of Science and the Social Order*, edited by Jasanoff, S. New York: Routledge, 13–45.

Jasco, P. (2005). "As We May Search: Comparison of Major Features of the Web of Science, Scopus, and Google Scholar Citation-Based and Citation-Enhanced Databases." *Current Science* 89.9: 1537–1547.

Jensen, F. (2007). *Introduction to Computational Chemistry*. West Sussex, England: John Wiley & Sons.

Juola, P. (2008). "Killer Applications in Digital Humanities." *Literary and Linguist Computing* 23.1: 73–83.

Kainz, C. (2010). *The Engine that Started Project Bamboo*. Available at: http://fridaysushi.com/2010/01/30/the-engine-that-started-project-bamboo/; accessed July 20, 2015.

Karp, R. M. (2011). "Heuristic Algorithms in Computational Molecular Biology." *Journal of Computer and System Sciences* 77.1: 122–128.

Kirschenbaum, M. (2012). "What Is Digital Humanities and What's It Doing in English Departments?" In *Debates in the Digital Humanities*, edited by Gold, M. K. Minneapolis: University of Minnesota Press, 3–11.

Kirschenbaum, M. (2014). "What Is 'Digital Humanities,' and Why Are They Saying Such Terrible Things about It?" *Differences* 25.1. Available at http://eadh.org/sites/default/files/dhterriblethingskirschenbaum.pdf, accessed July 20, 2014.

Knorr-Cetina, K. (1999). Epistemic Cultures: How the Sciences Make Knowledge. Cambridge, MA: Harvard University Press.

Knorr-Cetina, K., and Mulkay, M. (1983). *Science Observed: Perspectives on the Social Study of Science*. Beverly Hills, CA: Sage.

Kok, J., and Wouters, P. (2013). "Virtual Knowledge in Family History: Visionary Technologies, Research Dreams, and Research Agendas." In *Virtual Knowledge: Experimenting in the Humanities and the Social Sciences*, edited by Wouters, P., Beaulieu, A., Scharnhorst, A., and Wyatt, S. Cambridge, MA: MIT Press, 219–244.

Kortekaas, S. (2012). "Thinking the Unthinkable: A Library Without a Catalogue—Reconsidering the Future of Discovery Tools for Utrecht University Library." Association of European Research Libraries. Available at http://www.libereurope.eu/blog/thinking-the-unthinkable-alibrary-without-a-catalogue-reconsidering-the-future-of-discovery-tools, accessed July 28, 2014.

Latour, B. (1988). *Science in Action: How to Follow Scientists and Engineers through Society*. Cambridge, MA: Harvard University Press.

Latour, B., and Woolgar, S. (1986). *Laboratory Life: The Construction of Scientific Facts*. Princeton, NJ: Princeton University Press.

Law, J. (2004). *After Method: Mess in Social Science Research*. New York: Routledge.

Liu, A. (2009). "Digital Humanities and Academic Change." *English Language and Notes* 47: 17–35.

Liu, A. (2012). "Where Is Cultural Criticism in the Digital Humanities?" In *Debates in the Digital Humanities*, edited by Gold, M. K. Minneapolis: University of Minnesota Press, 490–510.

Liu, A. (2013). "The Meaning of the Digital Humanities." *PMLA* 128.2: 409–423.

Lord, R. D. (1958). "Studies in the History of Probability and Statistics: viii. de Morgan and the Statistical Study of Literary Style." *Biometrika* 45: 282.

Marshall, C. C. (2007). "How People Manage Personal Information over a Lifetime." In *Personal Information Management*, edited by Jones and Teevan. Seattle: University of Washington Press, pp. 57–75. Available at http://www.csdl. tamu.edu/~marshall/PIM%20Chapter-Marshall.pdf>, accessed November 18, 2014.

Marvin, C. (1988). *When Old Technologies Were New: Thinking about Electric Communication in the Late Nineteen Century.* New York and Oxford: Oxford University Press.

McCarthy Madsen, C. (2010). *Communities, Innovation, and Critical Mass: Understanding the Impact of Digitization on Scholarship in the Humanities through the Case of Tibetan and Himalayan Studies.* Thesis submitted in partial fulfilment of the requirements for the degree of DPhil in Information, Communication and the Social Sciences at the Oxford Internet Institute at the University of Oxford. Available at http://ora.ouls.ox.ac.uk/objects/uuid:928053ea-e8d9-44ff-9c9a-aaae1f6dc695, accessed July 20, 2014.

McCarty, W., and Short, H. (2002). "Mapping the Field." European Association of Digital Humanities. Available at http://www.eadh.org/mapping-field, accessed August 5, 2014.

McGann, J. (2002). *The Ivanhoe Game.* Available at http://www2.iath.virginia. edu/jjm2f/old/Igamesummaryweb.htm, accessed August 5, 2014.

McPherson, T. (2009). "Introduction: Media Studies and the Digital Humanities." *Cinema Journal* 48.2: 119–123.

Meyer, E. T., Eccles, K., Thelwall, M., and Madsen, C. (2009). Final Report to JISC on the Usage and Impact Study of JISC funded Phase 1 Digitisation Projects & the Toolkit for the Impact of Digitised Scholarly Resources (TIDSR). Available at http://microsites.oii.ox.ac.uk/tidsr/system/files/TIDSR_FinalReport_20July2009.pdf, accessed September 20, 2014.

Misa, T. J. (2009). "Findings Follow Framings: Navigating the Empirical Turn." *Synthese* 168: 357–375.

Mokyr, J. "Evolutionary Biology, Technological Change and Economic History." *Bulletin of Economic Research* 43.2: 127–149.

Morton, A. Q. (1965). *The Authorship of the Pauline Epistles: A Scientific Solution.* Saskatoon: University of Saskatchewan.

Nentwich. M. (2003). *Cyberscience: Research in the age of the Internet.* Vienna: Austrian Institute of Technology Assessment.

Neuhaus, C., Neuhaus, E., Asher, A., and Wrede, C. (2006). "The Depth and Breadth of Google Scholar: An Empirical Study. *portal: Libraries and the Academy* 6.2: 127–141.

Nicholas, D. (2010). "The Behaviour of the Researcher of the Future (the 'Google generation')." *Art Libraries Journal* 35.1: 18–21.

Nicholas, D., Rowlands, I., Huntington, P., Clark, D., and Jamali, H. (2009). "E-journals: Their Use, Value and Impact." *Research Information Network*, London. Available at http:// www.rin.ac.uk/system/files/attachments/E-journals-report.pdf, accessed August 5, 2014.

Nicholas, D., Rowlands, I., Williams, P., Brown, D., and Clark D. (2011). "E-journals: Their Use, Value and Impact—Final Report." Research Information Network, London. Available at http://www.rin.ac.uk/system/files/attachments/E-journals-report.pdf, accessed August 8, 2014.

Noble, D. (2002). "The Rise of Computational Biology." *Nature Reviews Molecular Cell Biology* 3.6: 459–463.

Norman, A. D. (1993). *Things That Make Us Smart: Defending Human Attributes in the Age of the Machine*. Cambridge, MA: Perseus.

Nowviskie, B. (2011). "Introduction: Two Tramps in Mud Time." In *#Alt-Academy: 01, Alternative Academic Careers for Humanities Scholars*, edited by Nowviskie, B. Available at http://mediacommons.futureofthebook.org/alt-ac/sites/mediacommons.futureofthebook.org.alt-ac/files/alt-academy01.pdf, accessed September 16, 2014.

Porsdam, H. (2013). "Digital Humanities: On Finding the Proper Balance between Qualitative and Quantitative Ways of Doing Research in the Humanities." *Digital Humanities Quarterly* 7.3. Available at http://www.digitalhumanities.org/dhq/vol/7/3/000167/000167.html, accessed July 5, 2014.

Posner, M. (2013). "No Half Measures: Overcoming Common Challenges to Doing Digital Humanities in the Library." *Journal of Library Administration* 53: 43–52.

Price, K. M. (2009). "Edition, Project, Database, Archive, Thematic Research Collection: What's in a Name?" *Digital Humanities Quarterly* 3.3. Available at http://www.digitalhumanities.org/dhq/vol/3/3/000053/000053.html, accessed August 5, 2014.

Purcell, K., Buchanan, J., and Friedrich, L. (2013). "The Impact of Digital Tools on Student Writing and How Writing is Taught in Schools." *Pew Research Internet Project*. Available at http://www.pewinternet.org/2013/07/16/the-impact-of-digital-tools-on-student-writing-and-how-writing-is-taught-in-schools/, accessed August 5, 2014.

Raley, R. (2014). "Digital Humanities for the Next Five Minutes." *Differences* 25.1: 26–45.

Ramsay, S. (2011). *Who's In and Who's Out*. Available at http://stephenramsay.us/text/2011/01/08/whos-in-and-whos-out/, accessed September 19, 2014.

Ramsay, S. (2013). *DH Types One and Two*. Available at http://stephenramsay.us/2013/05/03/dh-one-and-two/, accessed September 19, 2014.

Rheinberger, H. J. (1997). *Toward a History of Epistemic Things*. Stanford, CA: Stanford University Press.

Rogers, E. M. (2003/1962). *Diffusion of Innovations*. New York: Free Press.

Russell, D. B. (1967). *COCOA—A Word Count and Concordance Generator for Atlas*. Chilton: Atlas Computer Laboratory.

Scheinfeldt, T. (2010). *Where's the Beef? Does Digital Humanities Have to Answer Questions?* Available at http://foundhistory.org/2010/05/wheres-the-beef-does-digital-humanities-have-to-answer-questions/, accessed June 8, 2014.

Siemens, L. (2013). "Developing Academic Capacity in Digital Humanities: Thoughts from the Canadian Community." *Digital Humanities Quarterly* 7.1. Available at http://www.digitalhumanities.org/dhq/vol/7/1/000114/000114.html, accessed August 6, 2014.

Snow, C. P. (2012) [1959]. *The Two Cultures.* New York: Cambridge University Press.

Spiro, L. (2012). "'This is Why We Fight': Defining the Values of the Digital Humanities." In *Debates in the Digital Humanities*, edited by Gold, M. K. Minneapolis: University of Minnesota Press, 16–35.

Strathern, M. (2005). "Comment." *Current Anthropology* 46.3: 452–453.

Svensson, P. (2009). "Humanities Computing as Digital Humanities." *Digital Humanities Quarterly* 4.3. Available at http://www.digitalhumanities.org/dhq/vol/3/3/000065/000065.html, accessed July 20, 2014.

Svensson, P. (2010). "The Landscape of Digital Humanities." *Digital Humanities Quarterly* 4.1. Available at http://www.digitalhumanities.org/dhq/vol/4/1/000080/000080.html, accessed July 20, 2014.

Tenopir, C., King, D., and Bush, A. (2004). "Medical Faculty's Use of Print and Electronic Journals: Changes over Time and Comparison with Other Scientists." *Journal of the Medical Library Association* 92.2: 233–241.

Terras, M. (2012). *Quantifying Digital Humanities.* Available at http://blogs.ucl.ac.uk/dh/2012/01/20/infographic-quantifying-digital-humanities/, accessed July 18, 2014.

Thaller, M. (2012). "Controversies around the Digital Humanities: An Agenda." *Historical Social Research* 37.3: 7–23.

Unsworth, J. (2000). "Scholarly Primitives: What Methods Do Humanities Researchers Have in Common, and How Might Our Tools Reflect This?" Part of a Symposium on "Humanities Computing: Formal Methods, Experimental Practice, sponsored by King's College, London, May 13, 2000. Available at http://people.brandeis.edu/~unsworth/Kings.5-00/primitives.html, accessed July 20, 2014.

Unsworth, J. (2010). *The State of Digtial Humanities.* Available at http://people.brandeis.edu/~unsworth/state.of.dh.DHSI.pdf, accessed July 8, 2014.

Van Zundert, J., S. Antonijević, A. Beaulieu, K. van Dalen-Oskam, D. Zeldenrust, and T. Andrews. (2012). "Cultures of Formalization: Towards an encounter between humanities and computing." In *Understanding Digital Humanities: The Computational Turn and New Technology*, edited by David M. B. London: Palgrave Macmillan, 279–295.

Vanhoutte, E. (2013). "The Gates of Hell: History and Definition of Digital | Humanities | Computing." In *Defining Digital Humanities. A Reader*, edited by Terras, M., Nyhan, J., and Vanhoutte, E. Farnham: Ashgate, 119–156.

Wacquant, L. J. D. (1989). "Towards a Reflexive Sociology: A Workshop with Pierre Bourdieu." *Sociological Theory* 7.1: 26–63.

Waterman, M. S. (1995). *Introduction to Computational Biology: Maps, Sequences and Genomes.* Boca Raton, FL: CRC Press.

Winter, de J. C. F., Zadpoor, A. A., and Dodou, D. (2014). "The Expansion of Google Scholar versus Web of Science: A Longitudinal Study." *Scientometrics* 98: 1547–1565.

Wouters, P., Beaulieu, A., Scharnhorst, A., and Wyatt, S. (eds.). (2013). *Virtual Knowledge: Experimenting in the Humanities and the Social Sciences.* Cambridge, MA: MIT Press.

Wyatt, S., and Millen, D. (eds.). (2014). *Meaning and Perspectives in the Digital Humanities.* Amsterdam: Royal Netherlands Academy of Arts and Sciences.

Zastrow, J. (2014). "PIM 101: Personal Information Management." *Computers in Libraries*, 34.2, 22–24.

Zenil, H. (2011). "An Algorithmic Approach to Information and Meaning." Presented at the Interdisciplinary Workshop: Ontological, Epistemological and Methodological Aspects of Computer Science, Philosophy of Simulation (SimTech Cluster of Excellence), Institute of Philosophy, Faculty of Informatics, University of Stuttgart, Germany, July 7, 2011. Available at http://arxiv.org/pdf/1109.3887.pdf, accessed October 7, 2014.

Zorich, D. M. (2008). "Digital Humanities Centers: Loci for Digital Scholarship." In CLIR, *Working Together or Apart: Promoting the Next Generation of Digital Scholarship.* Washington, DC: Council on Library and Information Resources, 70–78. Available at http://www.clir.org/pubs/resources/promoting-digital-scholarship-ii-clir-neh/zorich.pdf, accessed July 5, 2014.

Zundert van, J., Antonijevic, S., Beaulieu, A., van Dalen-Oskam, K. H., Zeldenrust, D., and Andrews. T. (2012). "Cultures of Formalization: Towards an Encounter between Humanities and Computing." In *Understanding Digital Humanities: The Computational Turn and New Technology*, edited by David M. Berry. London: Palgrave Macmillan, 279–295.

4Humanities. (undated). "Mission." Available at http://4humanities.org/mission/, accessed October 7, 2014.

Index

CPSIA information can be obtained
at www.ICGtesting.com
Printed in the USA
LVOW04*2159050516

486942LV00014B/91/P